Whidbey: My Eye
A Whidbey Island Photogaphic Journal

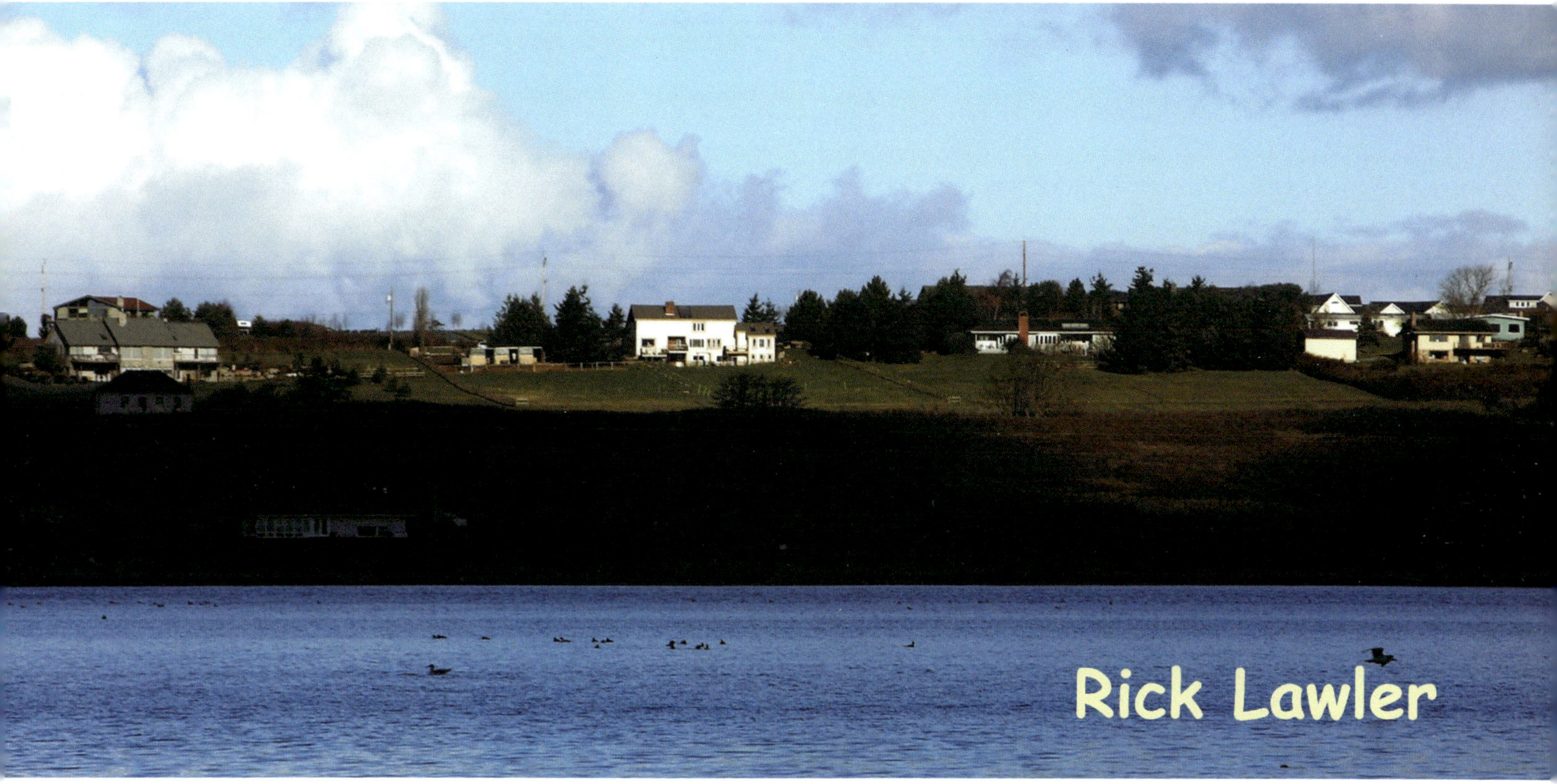

Rick Lawler

Copyright © 2007
by
Rick Lawler

All Rights Reserved

Printed in the U.S.A.
ISBN 978-1-930322-10-3

No part of this book may be reproduced or transmitted in any form or by any means, electronic, graphic, optical, or mechanical, including photocopying, recording, taping, electronic data, internet packets, or by any other information storage or retrieval method without written permission of the publisher. For information, contact MinRef Press, 2248 SW Vista Park Drive, Oak Harbor, WA 98277, minref@gmail.com

The opinions expressed in this book are those of the author. Mention or photos of persons, businesses or institutions does not imply endorsement of this book by mentioned or photographed persons, businesses or institutions.

This book is dedicated to
Shau Ying for having patience of Biblical proportions, for encouragement, and for being there, and for Sara and Sean for their encouragement and forgiveness.

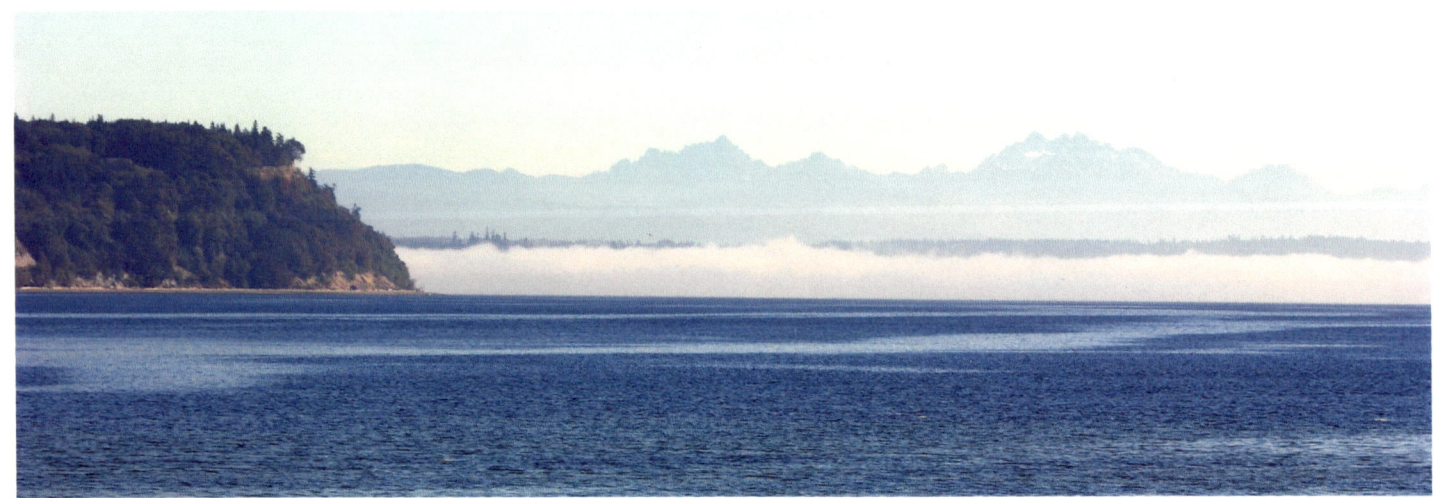

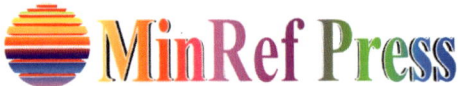

Introduction

This is not a comprehensive photographic representation of Whidbey Island. The island's natural resources and photographic subjects are simply too numerous and diverse for a small photo book such as this.

The photos, therefore, represent Whidbey as seen through my eye. Each photographer has his or her specialties and strengths. I don't usually do well with portraits or architectural photography, but better with landscapes and scenery, and I sometimes get lucky with closeups.

We moved to Whidbey in mid-2005 through an unlikely chain of fortunate events. Everyone – and I mean *everyone* – warned us about the rain. Others, more geographically challenged, simply assumed that living on an island was a throwback to primitive times. Sort of like the *Beverly Hillbillies* before they got rich, but without the accents and with a lot more water.

Reality, of course, paints a much nicer picture. I hope this book helps dispel some of the common myths of the Pacific Northwest. Not enough to make all my friends and relatives want to move here; just enough to make them all want to visit.

This is a personal journal, and I've tried to make it a fun trip. Hope you enjoy it!

Note: Some of the photos in this book may look suspiciously like paintings. Even so, they all started life as photographs.

While not exactly lies, technology gives wannabe artists such as myself an opportunity to convert a photograph into a close facsimile of a painting or drawing.

An example is the photo of downtown Coupeville to the right. I hope it fooled you into thinking I had great artistic talent.

Rick Lawler, Oak Harbor, Washington

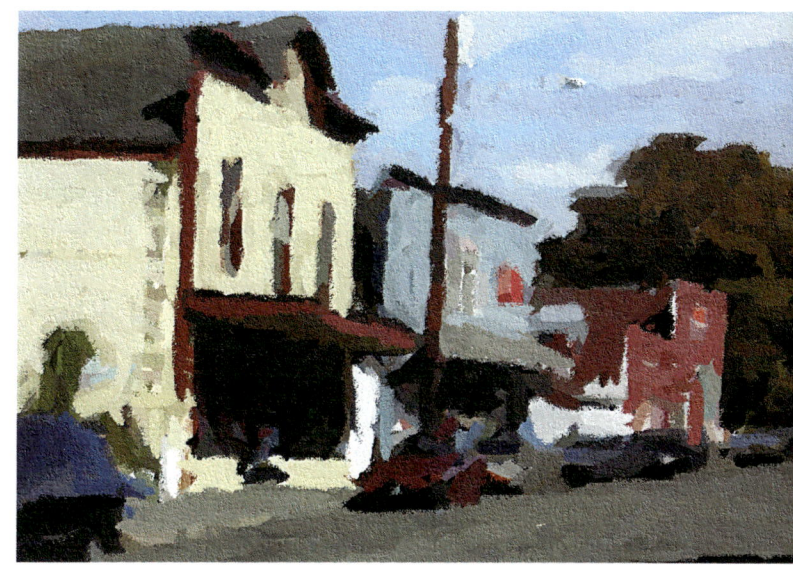

Deception Pass State Park

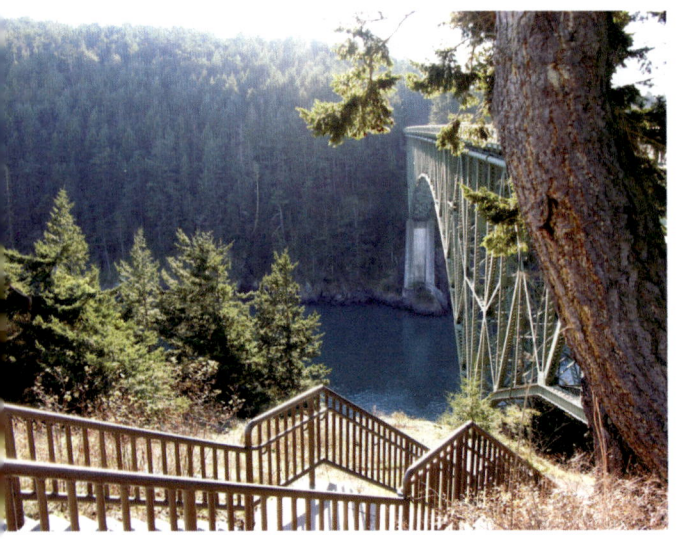

Deception Pass State Park marks the extreme Northern end of Whidbey Island.

The Deception Pass Bridge connects Whidbey Island with Fidalgo Island, and thus to the mainland. It is one of the top tourist stops in the Pacific Northwest.

Majestic old growth forests, hiking trails, sandy beaches, and Cranberry Lake make Deception Pass State Park a popular destination.

For more information on this picturesque State Park, log on to: www.parks.wa.gov

Photo of Deception Pass Bridge (Above) taken December, 2005; Deception Pass State Park (Below) taken March, 2006; and (Facing Page) another view of the bridge taken March, 2006.

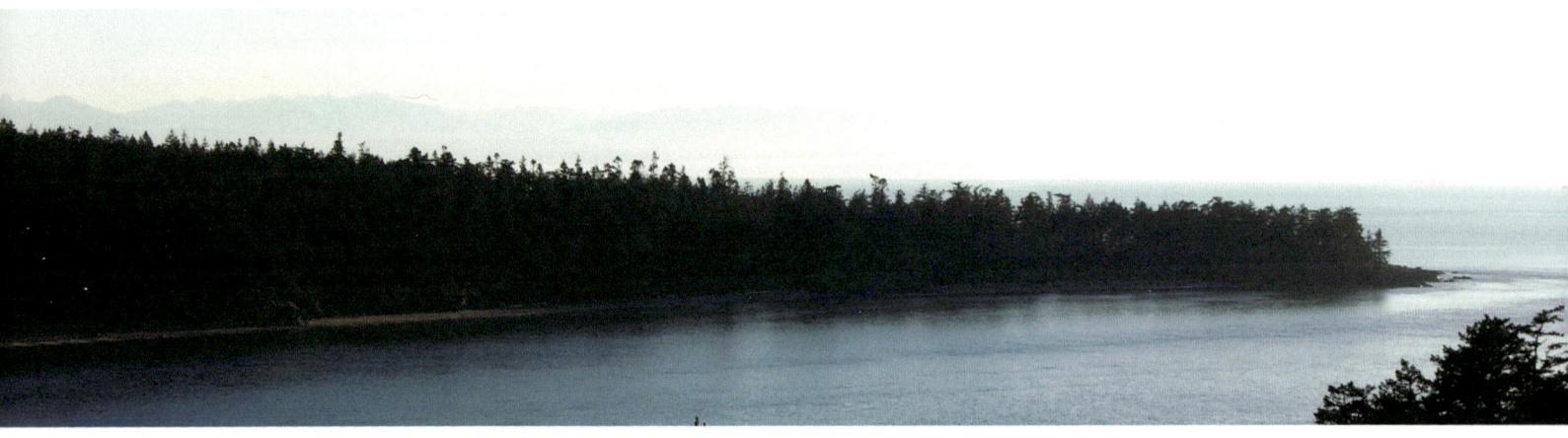

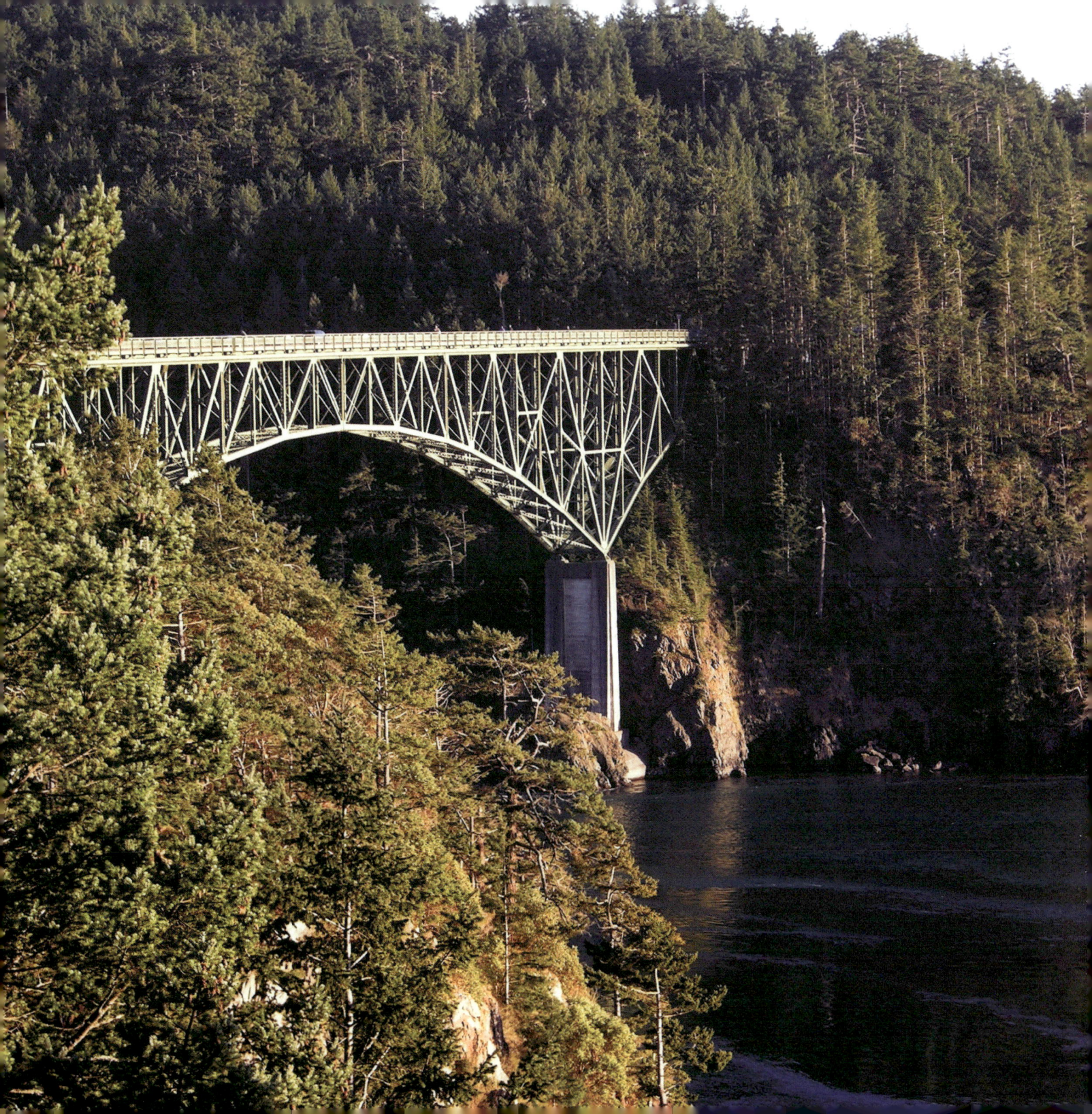

Cornet Bay

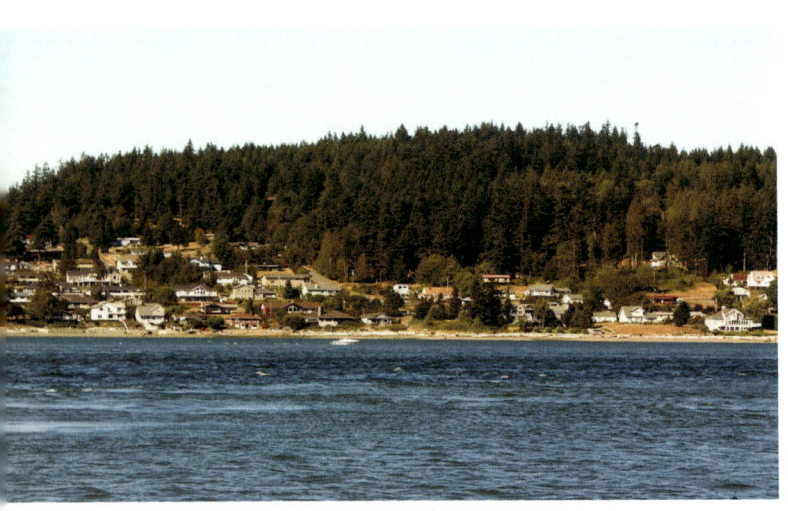

Cornet Bay is one of my favorite places. The views are spectacular from the Cornet Bay Marina.

This area is also the location of the Northeastern portion of Deception Pass State Park.

Beaches, views and hiking trails are the rewards of this peaceful and tranquil location. On a clear day, you'll see awesome views of Mt. Baker.

View of Fidalgo island (above) taken Sept. 2006; Cornet Bay and Mt. Baker (below) taken Sept. 2006; and a view of Cornet Bay (Facing Page) taken Feb. 2006.

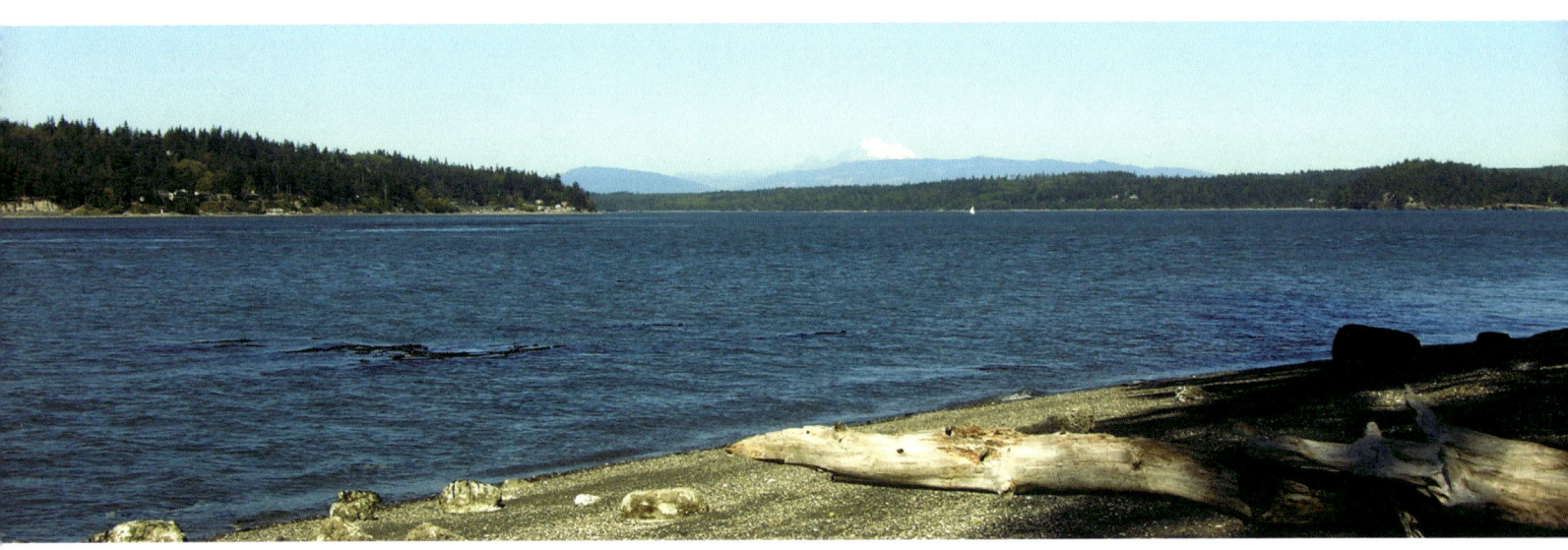

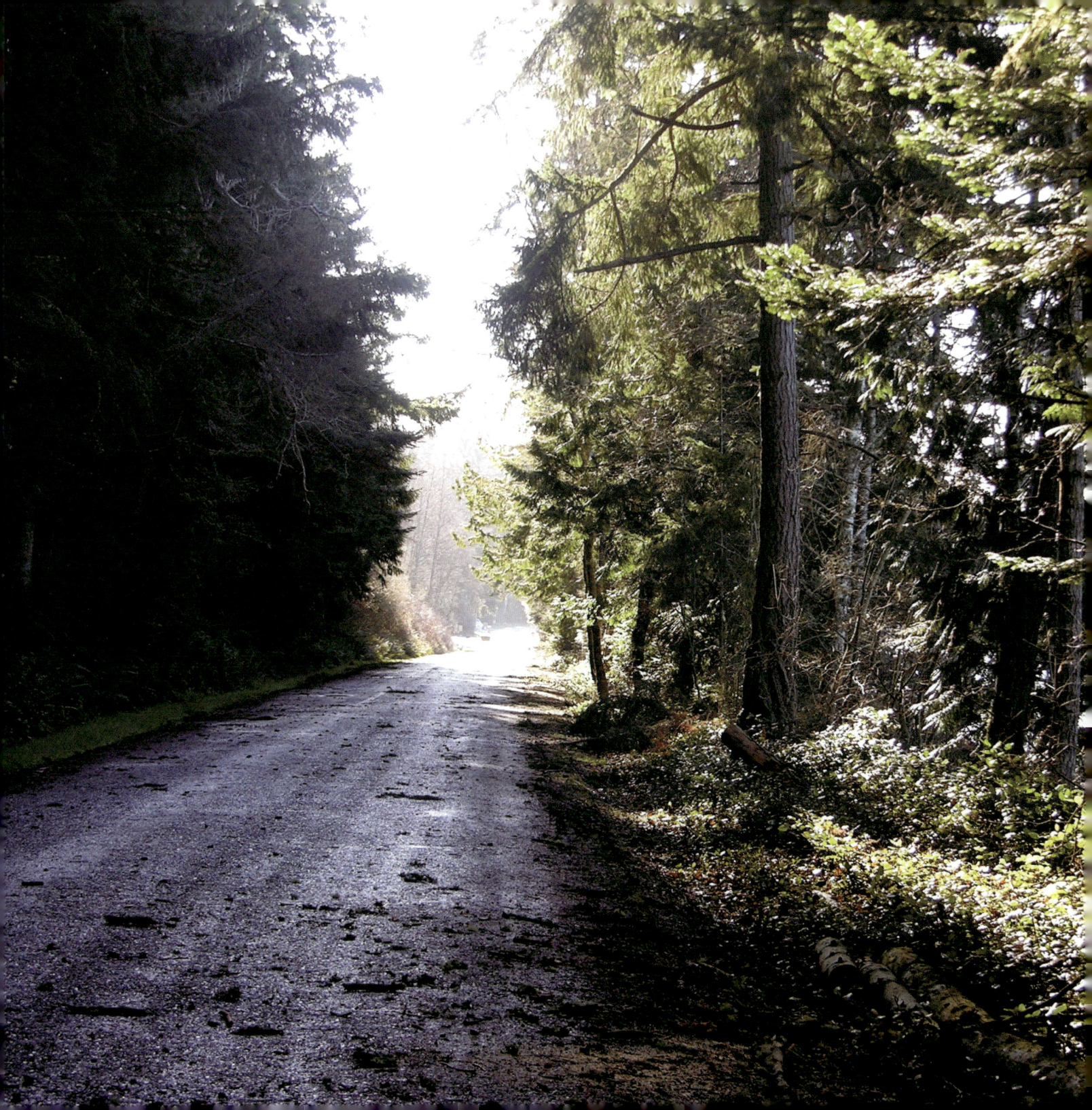

Oak Harbor

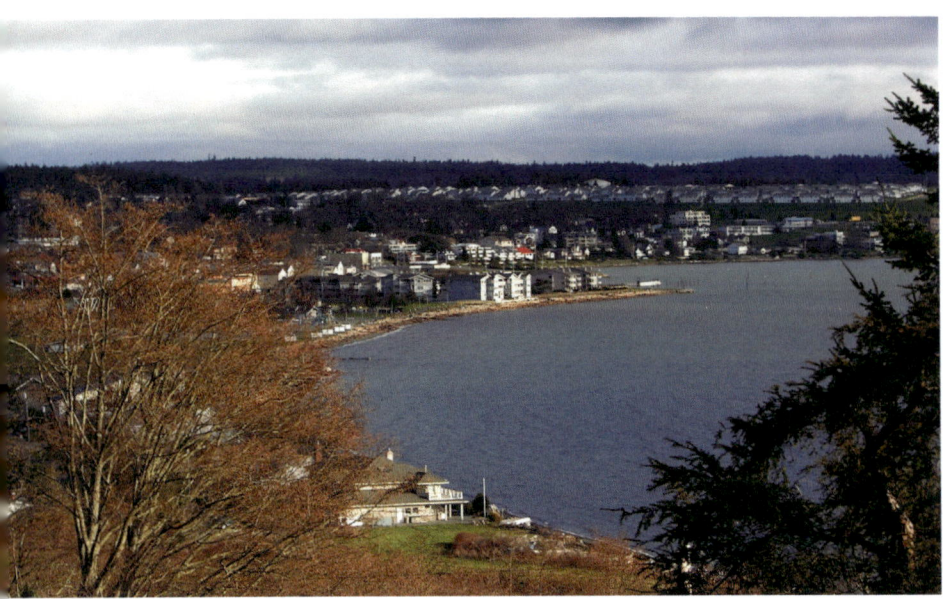

Oak Harbor is our home. The largest city on Whidbey Island, it offers most (if not all) the amenities that are considered necessities by the modern 21st Century human.

Despite its population base, Oak Harbor remains relatively compact. Here you will find quaint shops, parks, museums, a Navy base, big box retailers, the fast-food staples, accommodations, excellent restaurants, and much more.

The people are friendly, and crime rate low, the Island Transit bus service is free, and the library is open seven days a week during the school year. What more could you ask?

Photo of Oak Harbor downtown (above) taken Jan. 2006; Portion of Maylor Point (below) taken Feb. 2006; Oak Harbor Marina (facing page) taken Feb. 2006.

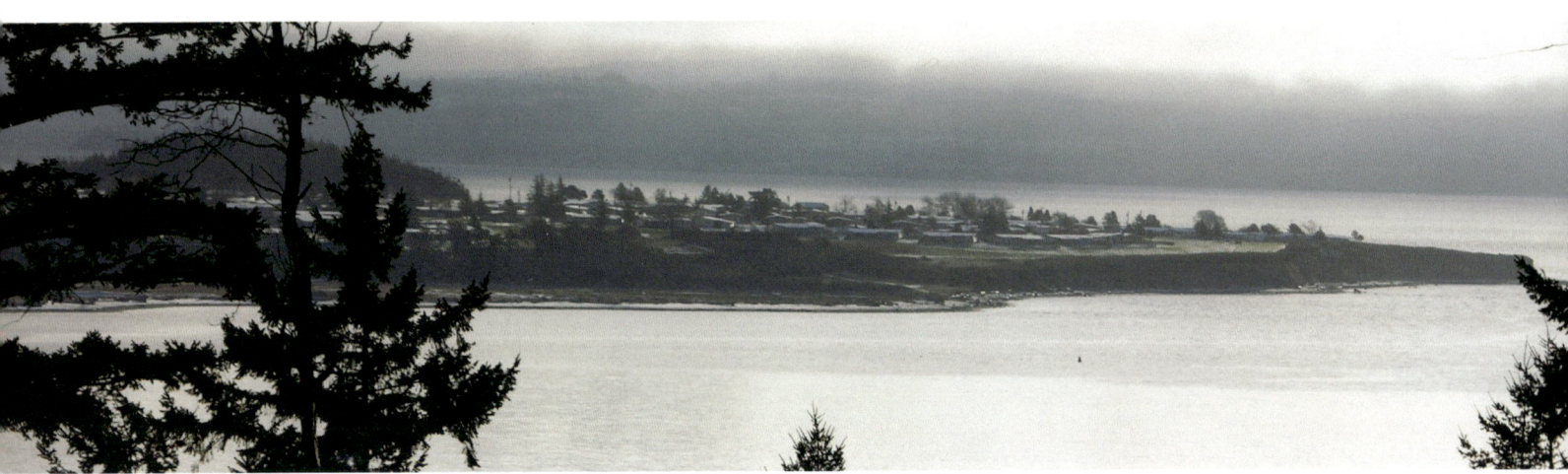

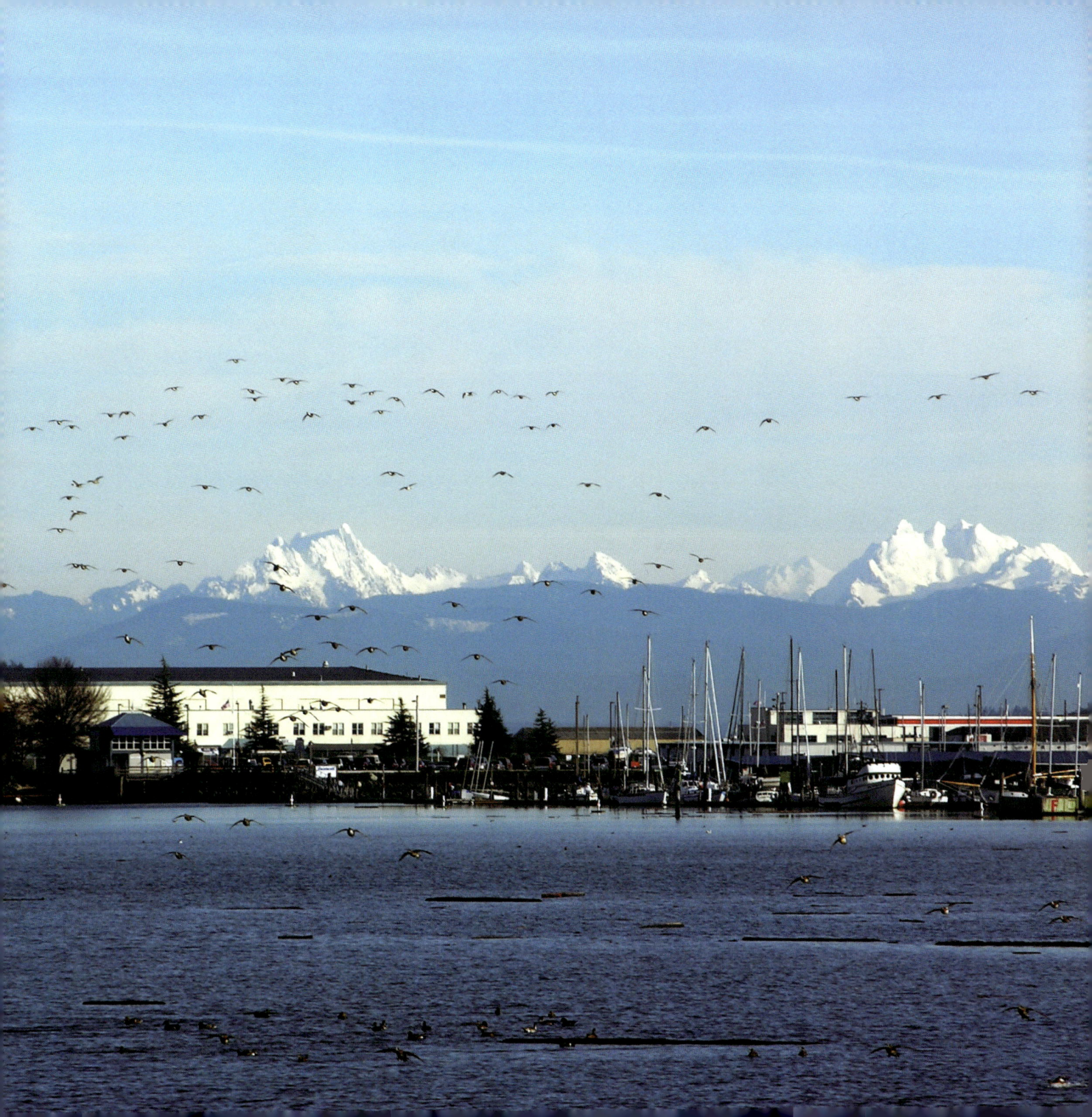

Oak Harbor

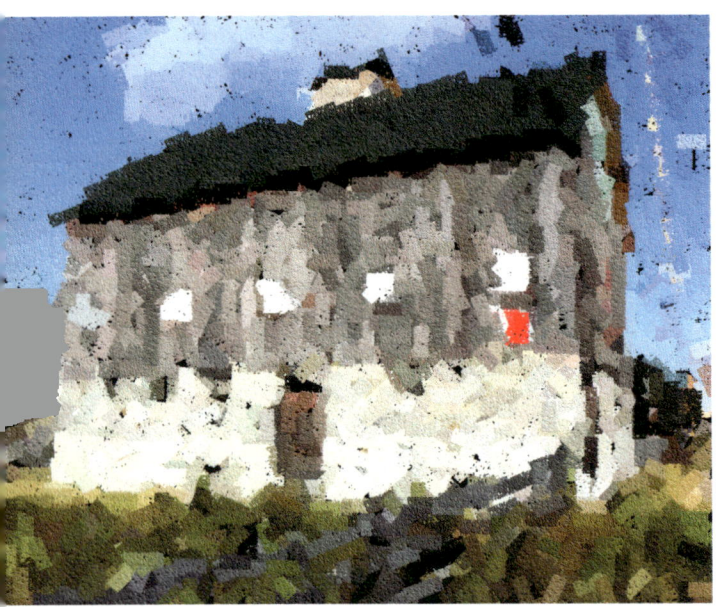

Oak Harbor is a city that has its roots in the rural countryside. It's not unusual to see an eagle fly overhead. You don't have to drive far to see farms and ranches, barns and tractors.

Whidbey is surrounded by tall mountains. On a clear day, it can seem those mountains are close enough to touch.

Take a deep breath, you city dwellers. That odd smell is called fresh air.

Historic building (above) taken Sept. 2006; Barn (below) taken Sept. 2006; Oak Harbor (facing page) taken Jan. 2006

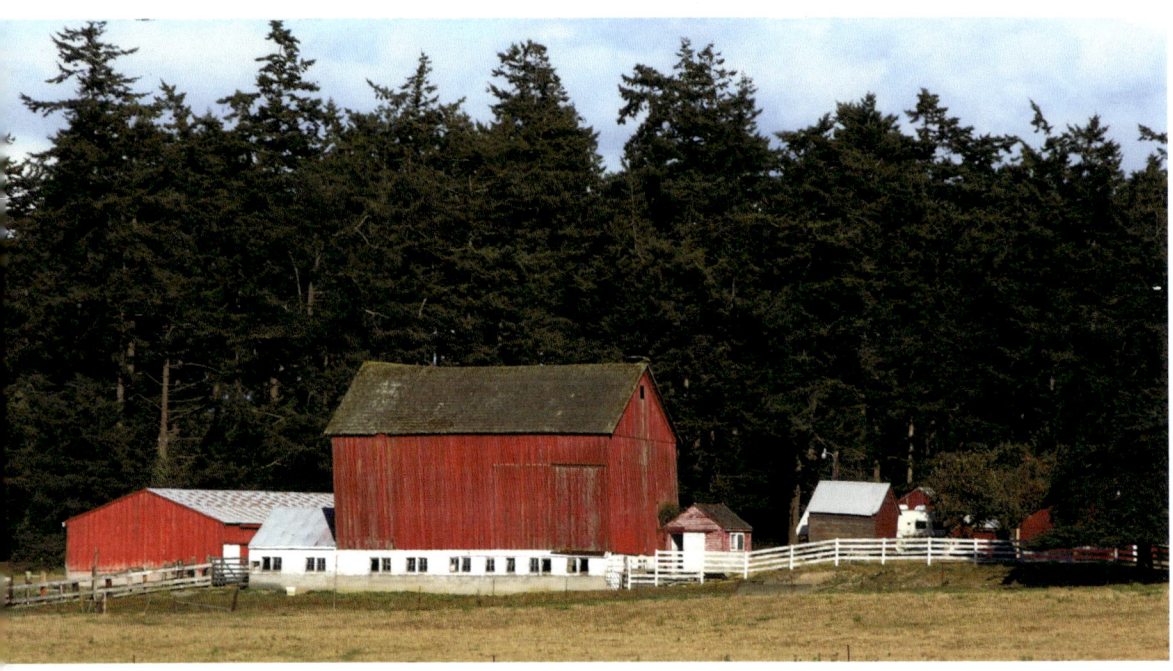

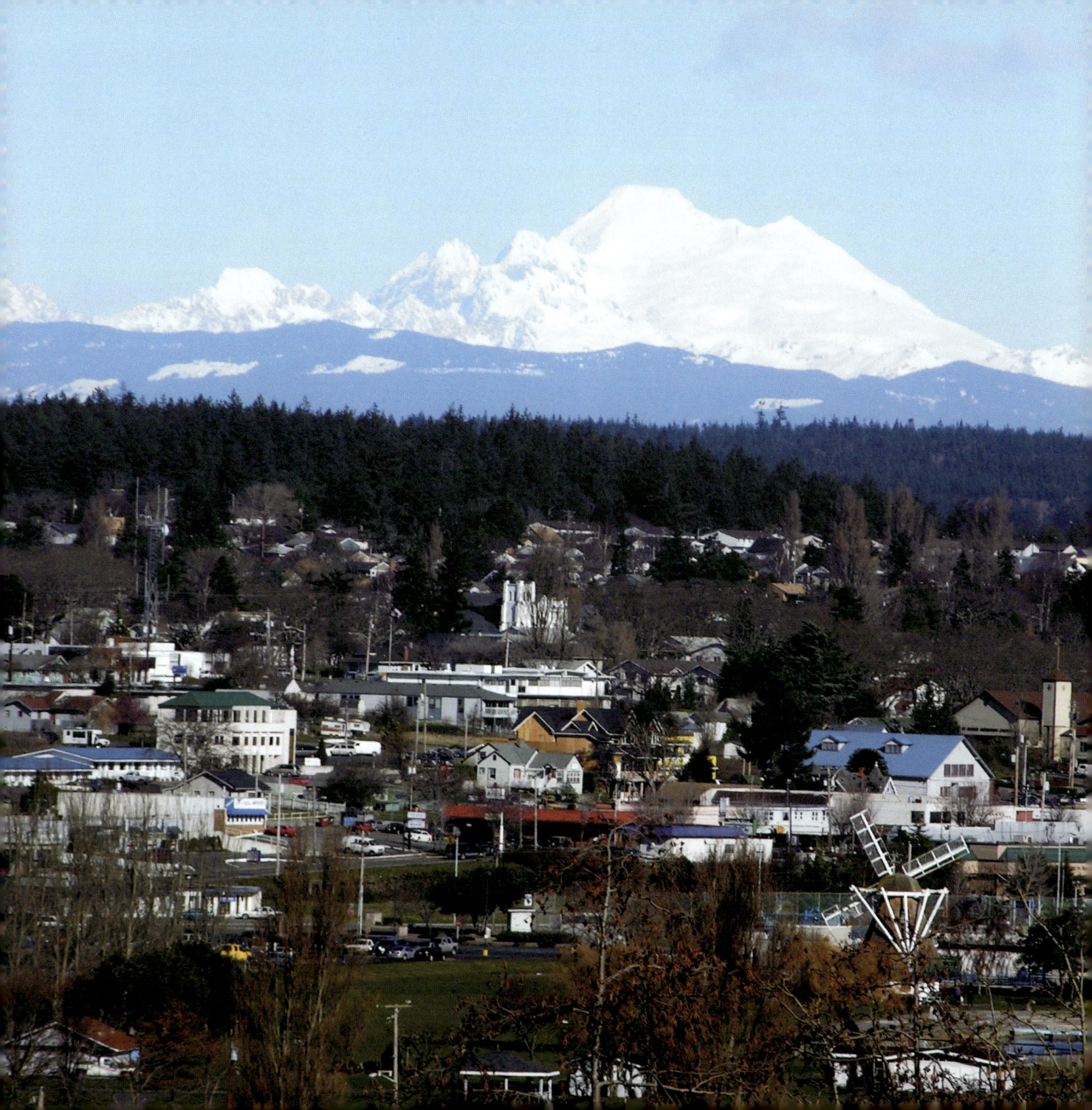

Joseph Whidbey State Park

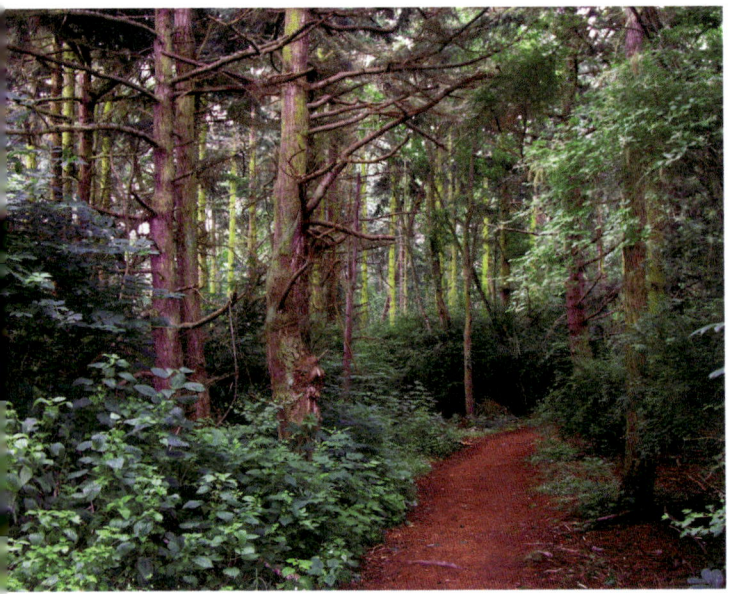

Joseph Whidbey State Park is located West of Oak Harbor. Just a few miles away from traffic lights, shopping carts, souvenir shops, and the tantalizing smells of restaurants, you will find peaceful hiking trails and lapping waves.

Stroll along the beach, gaze out at the San Juan Islands, let your cares drift away.

Even during peak tourist season, you'll sometimes find yourself the only one on the trail. Imagine that!

Joseph Whidbey State Park trail (above) taken June, 2006; beach (below) taken Feb. 2006; storm clouds (facing page), taken Oct. 2005

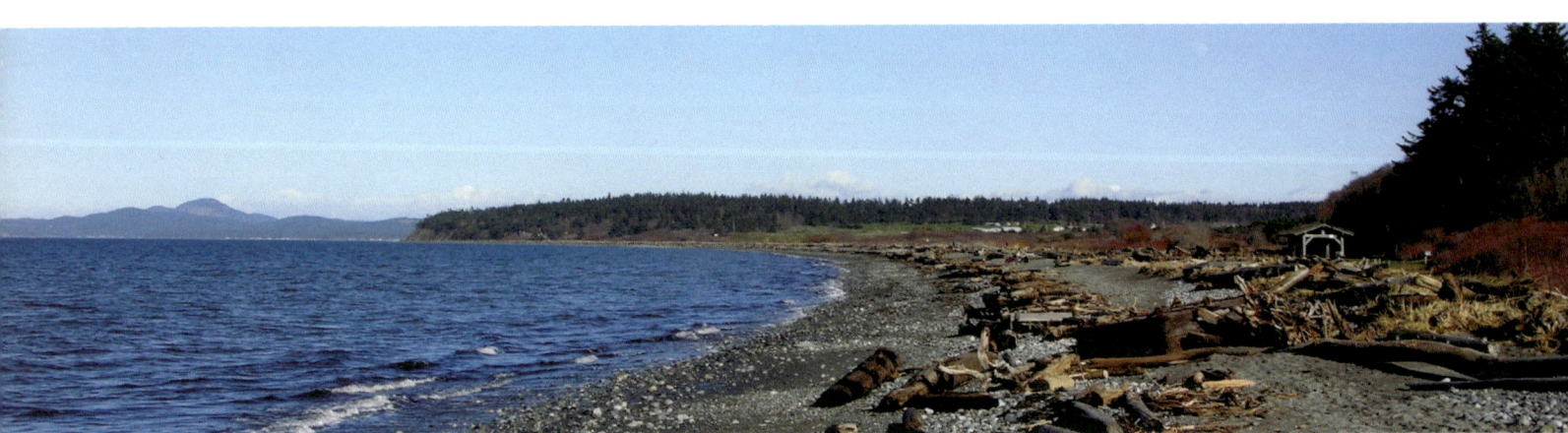

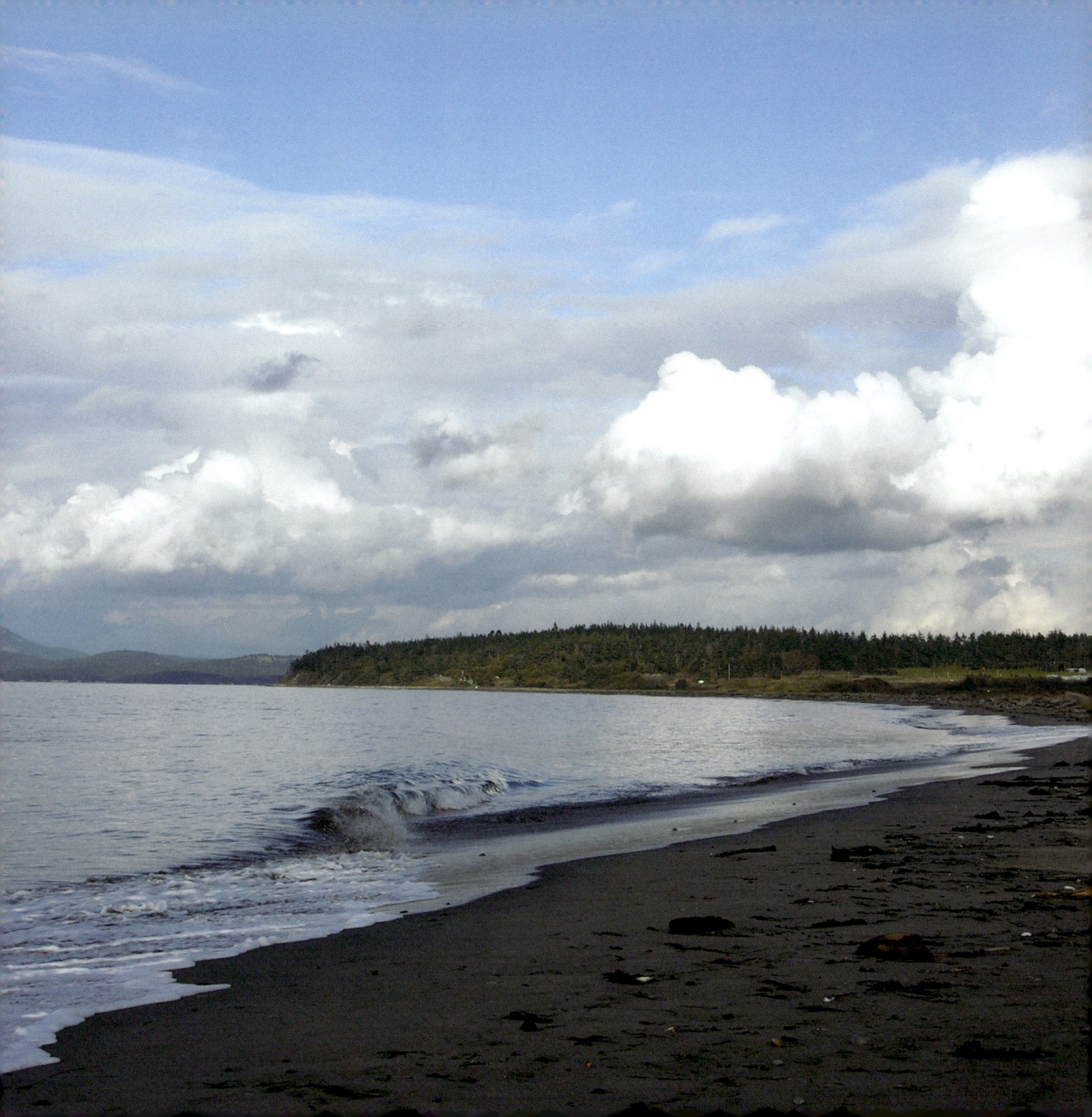

Ebey's Landing Historic Preserve

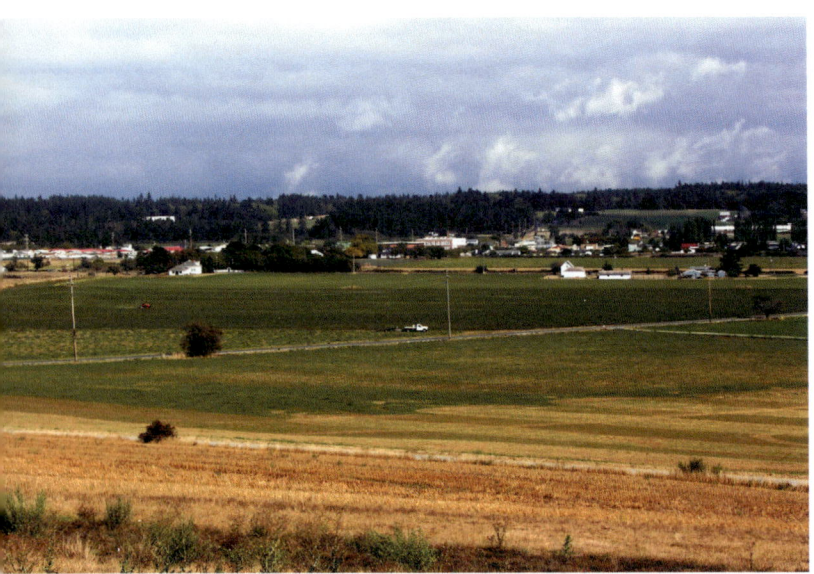

Ebey's Landing farms (above) taken Sept. 2006; prairie (below) taken Sept. 2006; cultivated fields (facing page) taken Sept. 2006.

Ebey's Landing Historic Preserve was established in the late 1970s to protect the rural and pastoral landscape.

The Preserve encompasses 17,000 acres of Central Whidbey and is part of the National Park System even though most of the land is privately owned.

For more information, visit: www.nps.gov/ebla/

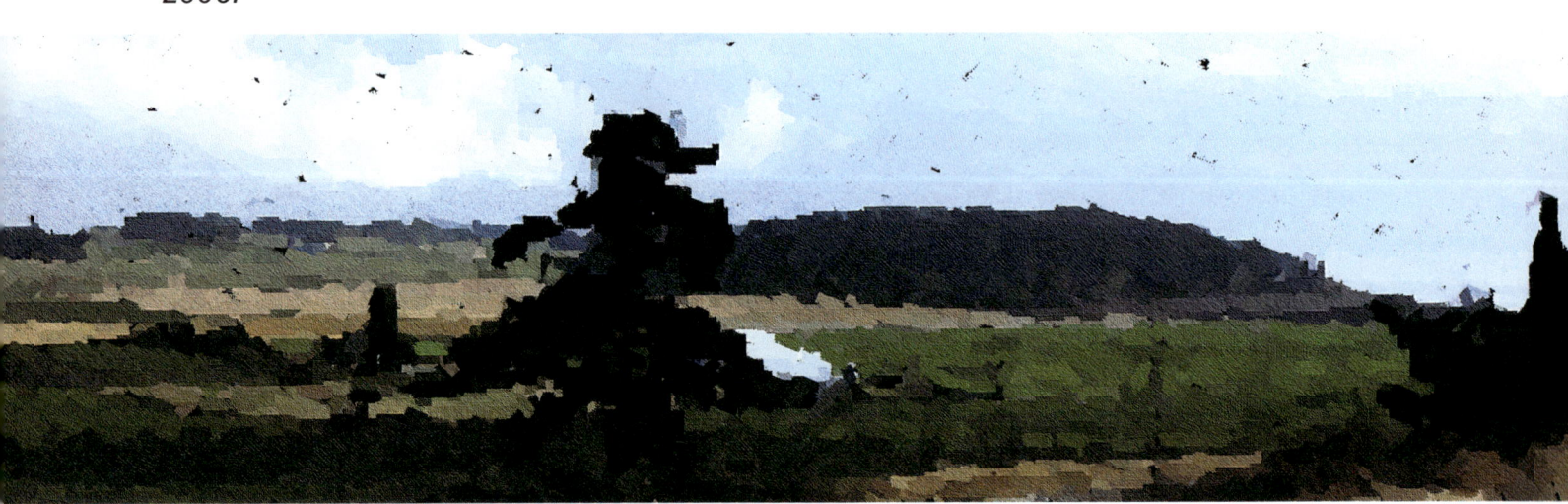

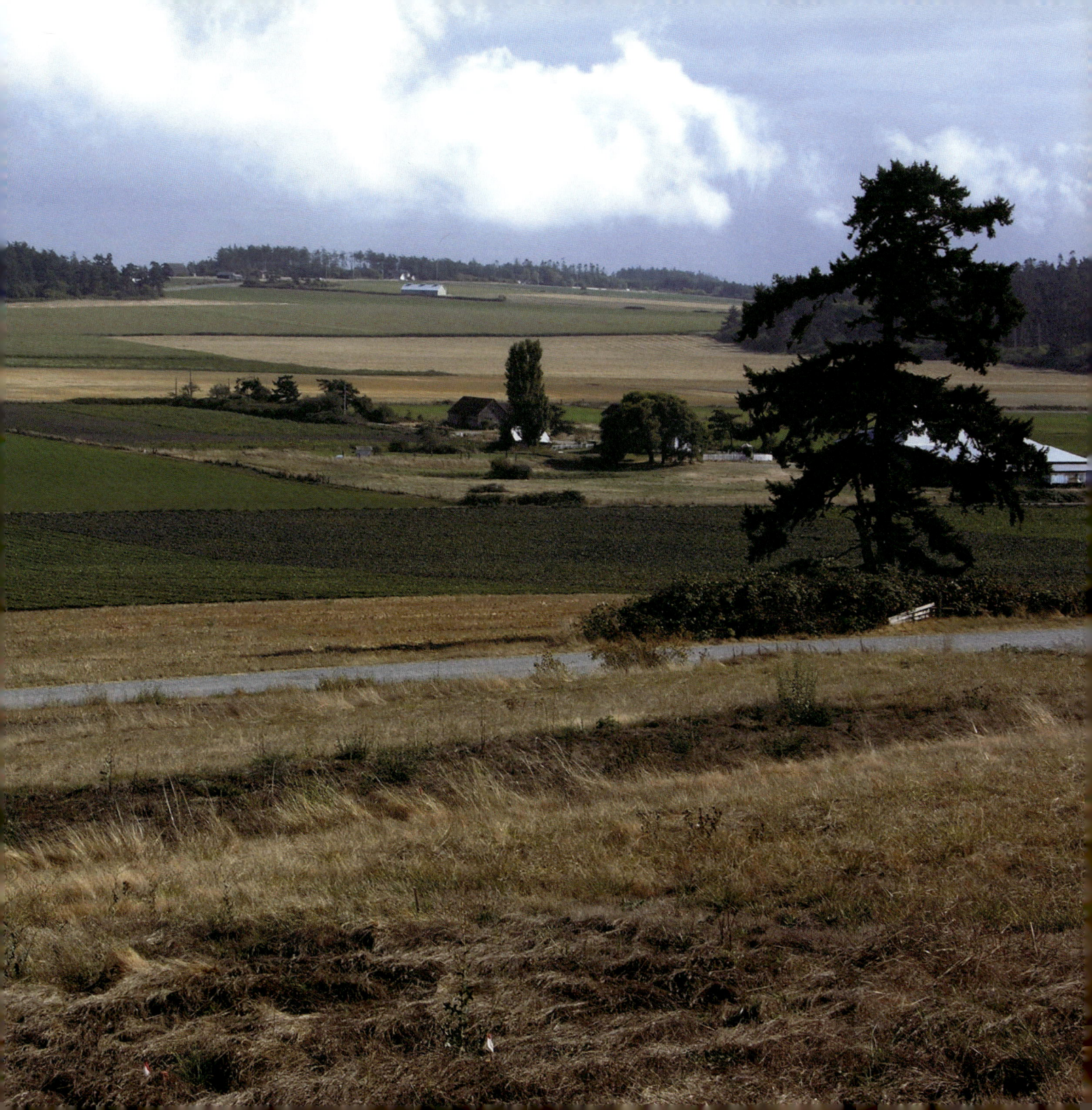

Coupeville

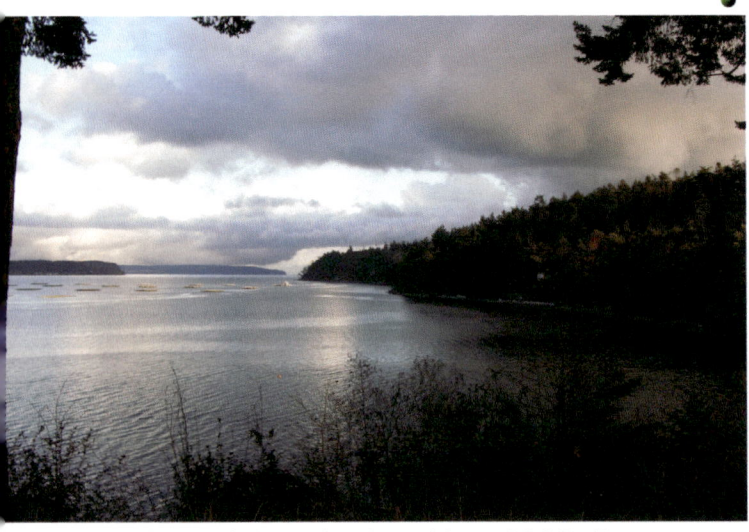

Coupeville is located on the South edge of Penn Cove. It is a town steeped in history, illuminated with historic buildings.

Coupeville is the seat of Island County government, the home of many artists and art galleries, fine dining, and beds and breakfasts of distinction.

There is something very special and timeless about Coupeville. Walking down Front Street, exploring the shops, time is frozen.

Penn Cove (above) taken Nov. 2005; Downtown (below, left) taken Sept. 2006; Spring flowers (below, center) taken March 2006, Historic Buildings (below, right) taken Sept. 2006; Wharf (facing page) taken March 2006

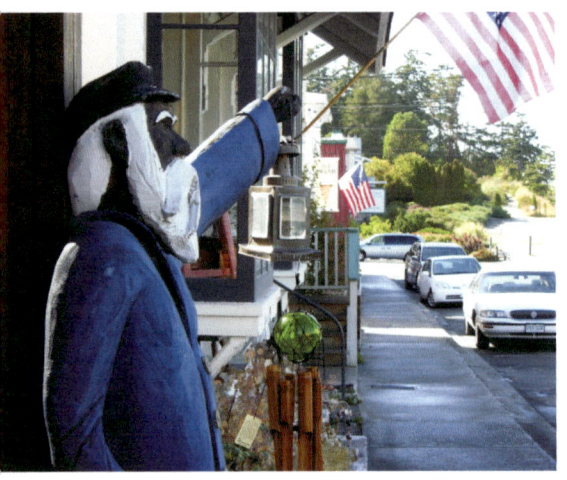
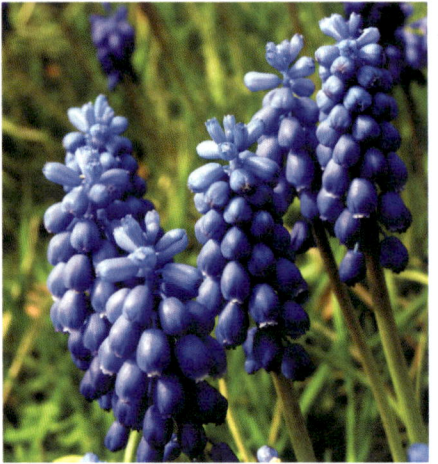
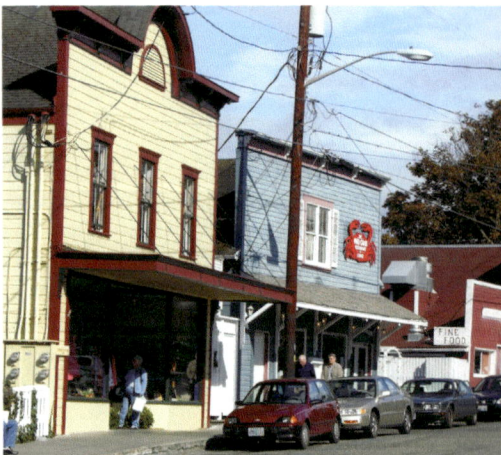

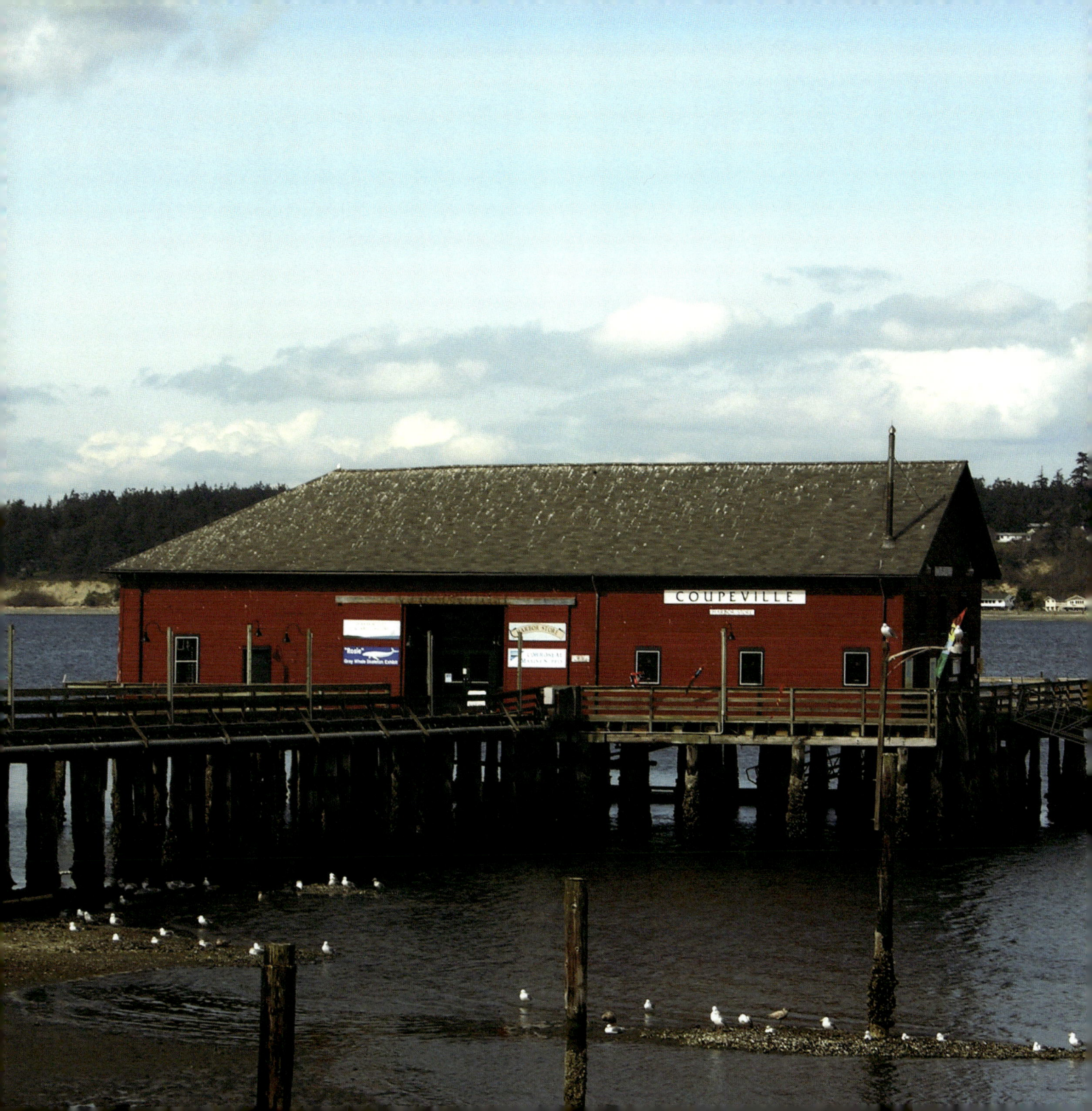

Race Week -- Penn Cove

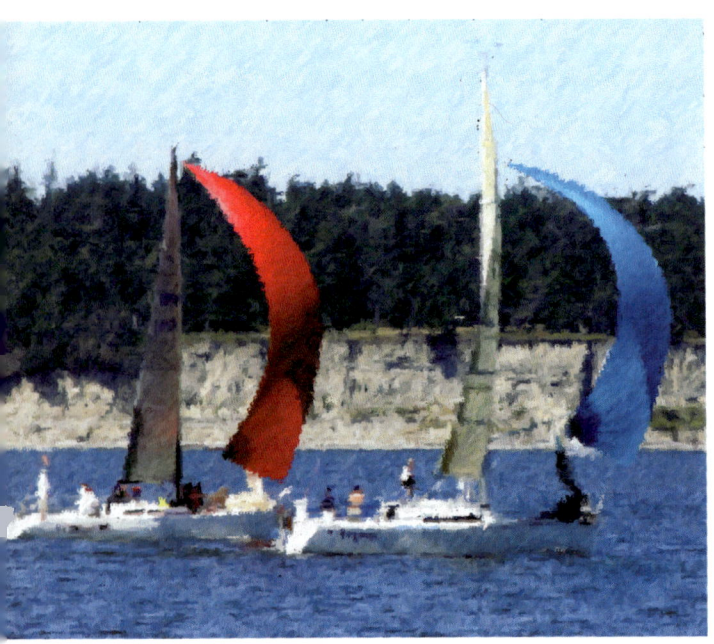

Race week is an annual regatta that takes place each July in Penn Cove. Just as Coupeville comes alive with a festive atmosphere, the Cove comes alive with hundreds of brightly-colored sailboats.

I suppose someone cares there's a race on, and that there are winners and losers. But judging from the smiles all around, that's the least important aspect of a fun and spectacular week.

This is an event not to be missed!

Race Week photos (above, below and facing page) taken July 2006 near Coupeville.

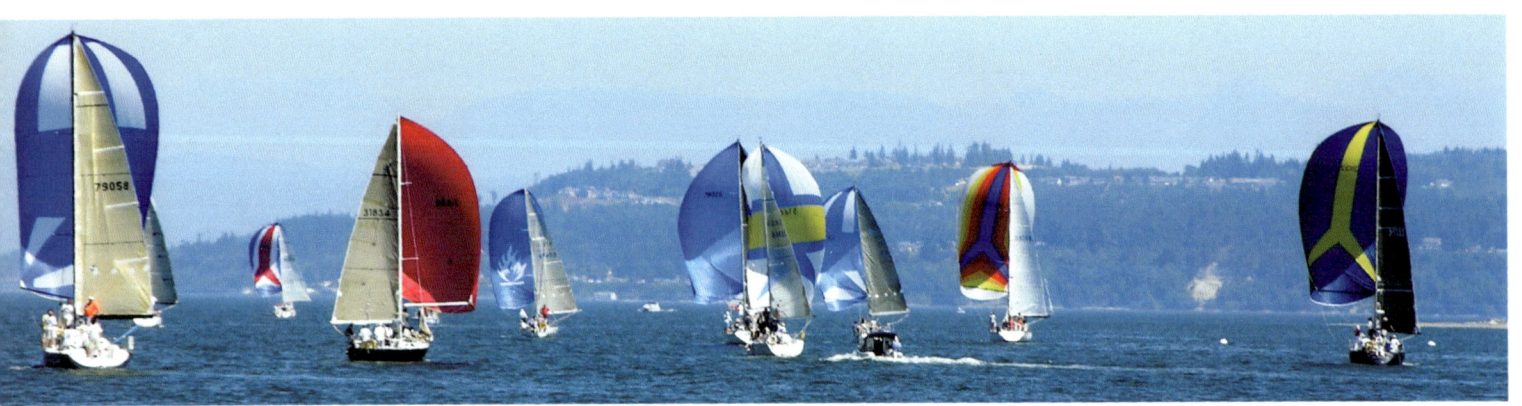

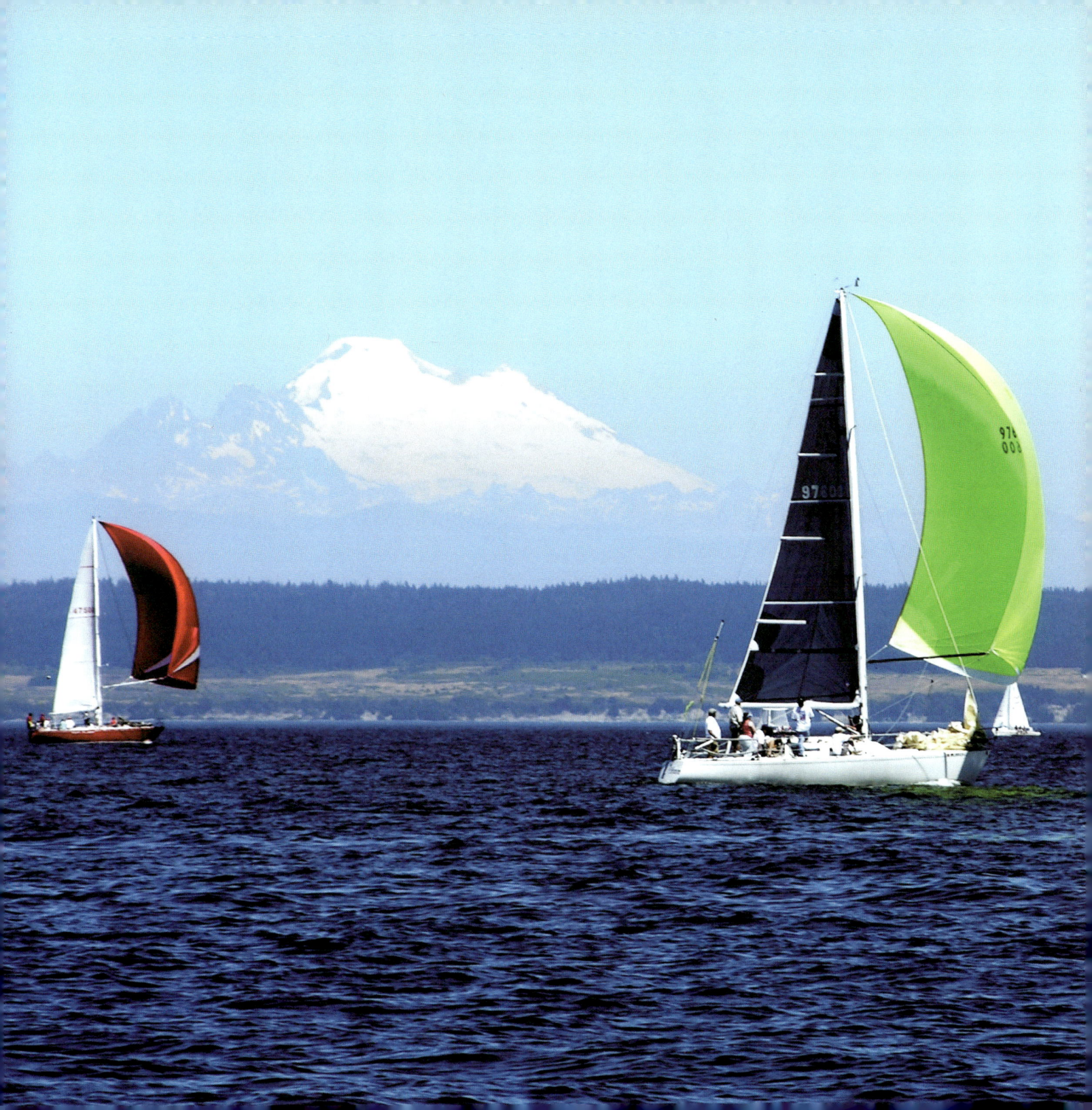

Race Week -- Penn Cove

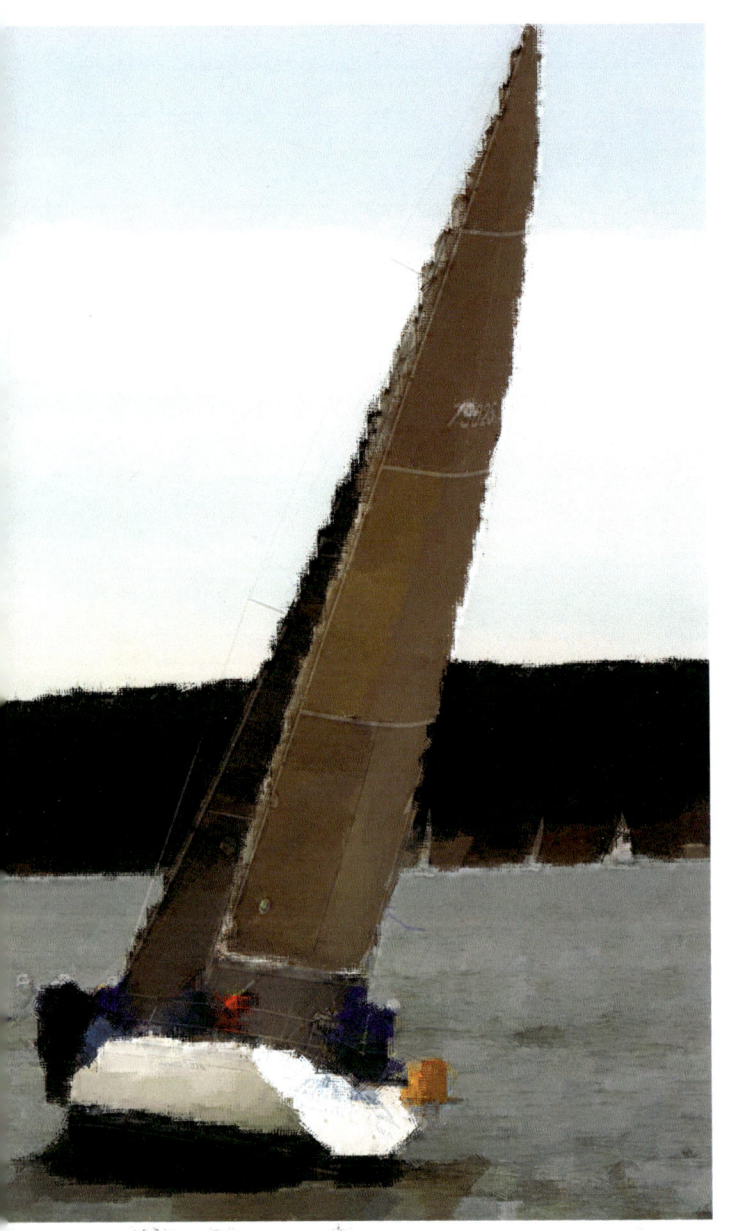

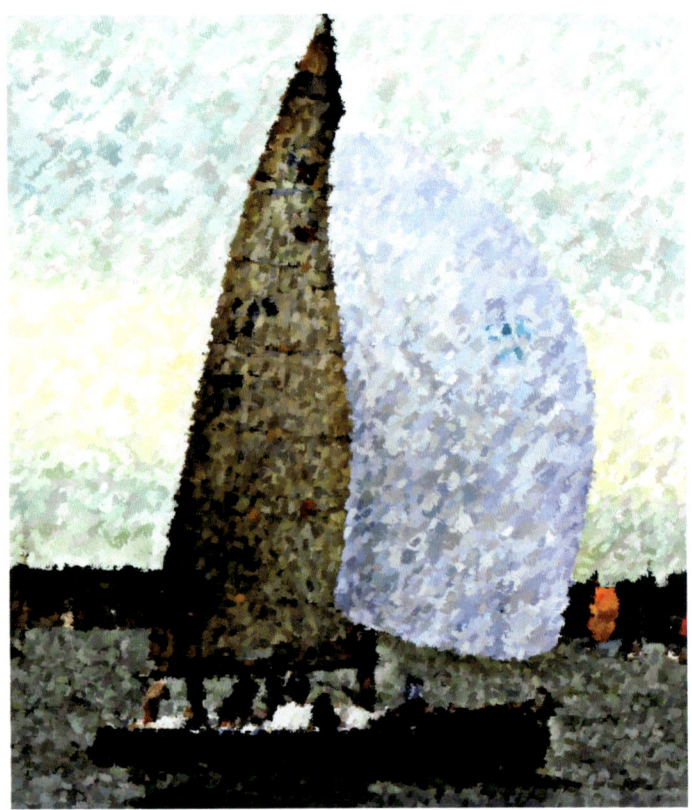

For more information on Race Week and other Coupeville-area events, log on to: www.centralwhidbeychamber.com or www.whidbey.com/raceweek

Race Week photos (left, above, facing page) taken July 2006.

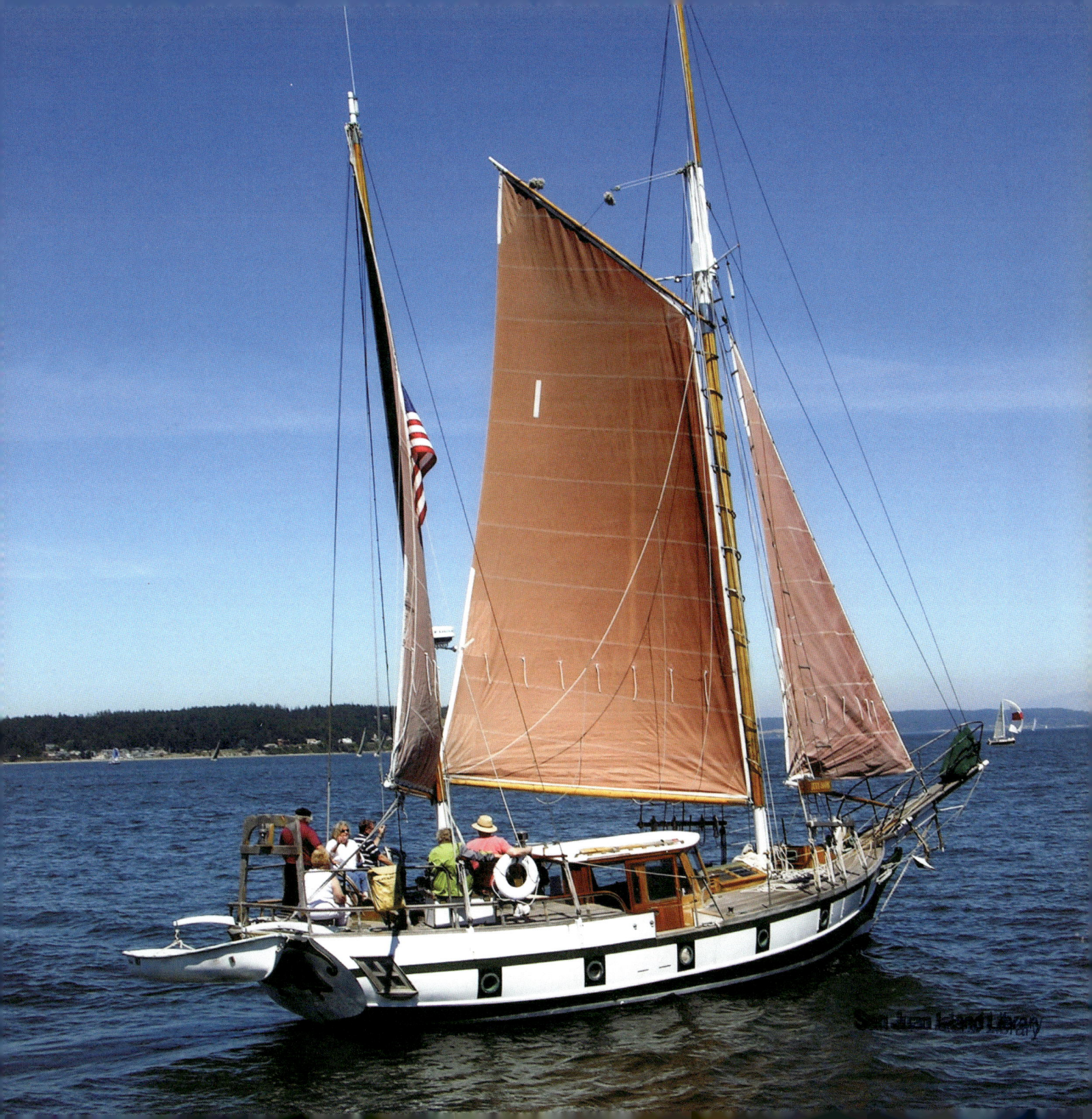

Ft. Casey Lighthouse

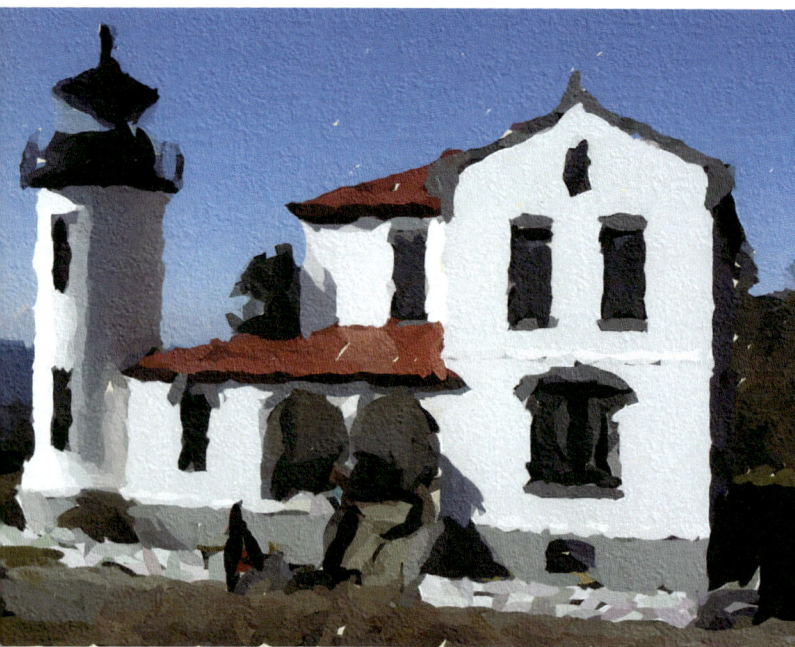

The Ft. Casey Lighthouse is one of the most photographed buildings on Whidbey Island. It was originally built in 1861 and rebuilt in 1903, and now houses a museum. It was last used as a lighthouse in 1922.

The lighthouse is part of Ft. Casey State Park where there are displays of Admiralty Head's big guns and other remnants of its proud military past.

Today, you'll see deer, eagles, and kites. And some of the most awesome scenery in the world.

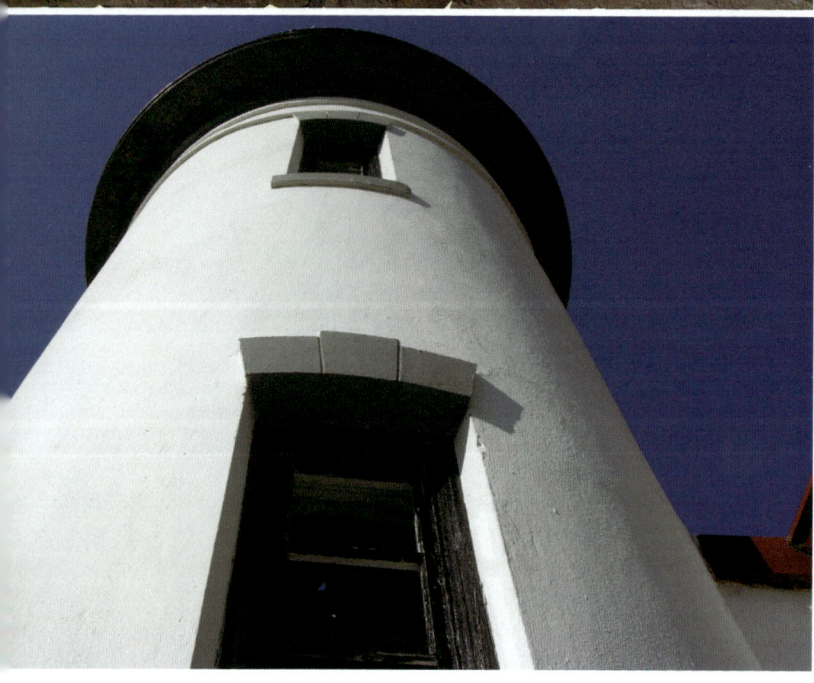

Ft. Casey Lighthouse photos (above left, left, and facing page) were taken March, 2006.

San Juan Island Library

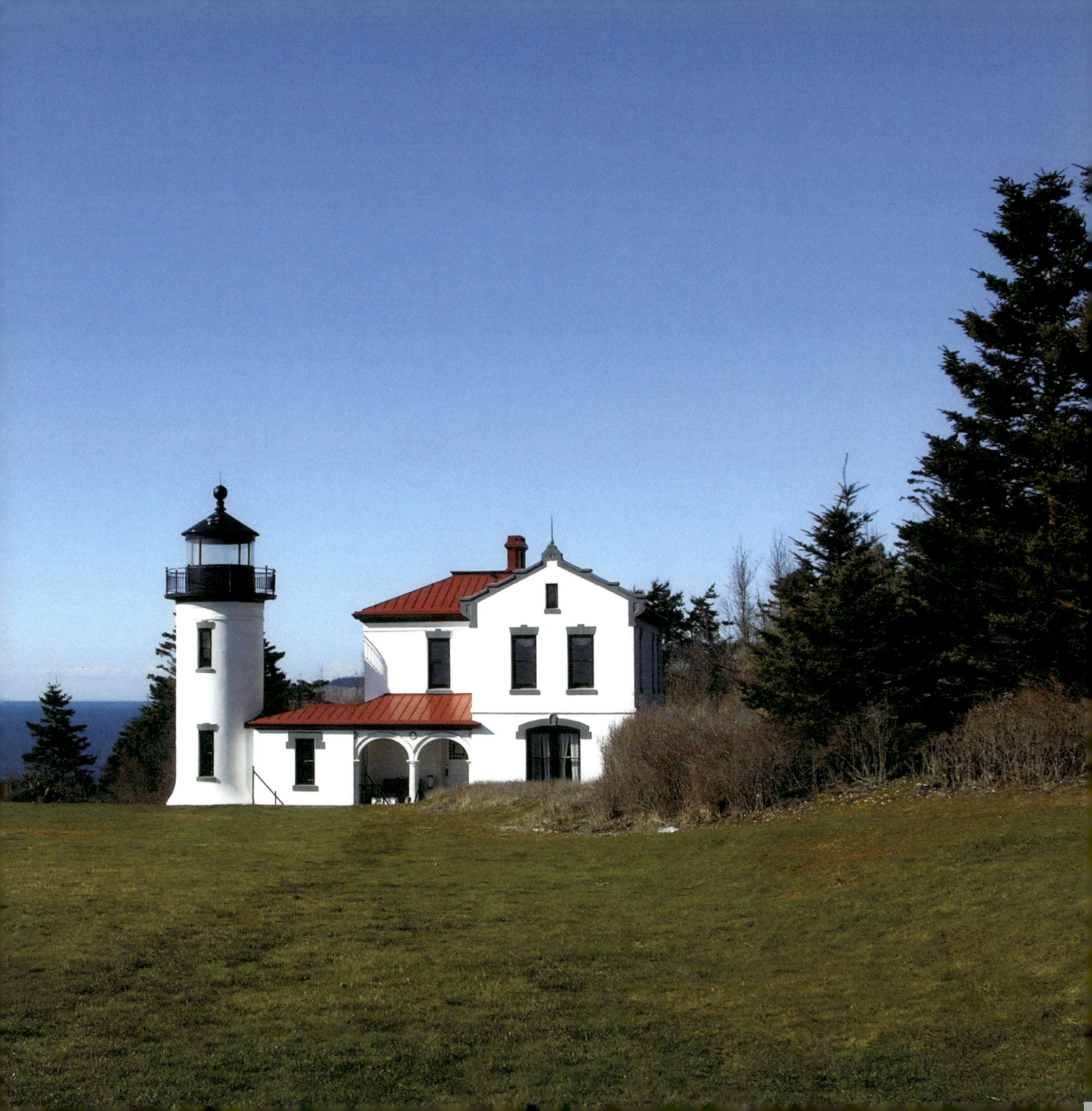

Ft. Casey State Park

Ft. Casey State Park is home not only to the Lighthouse and the big gun emplacements, it's also the location of Seattle Pacific University's Camp Casey Conference Center.

Once an Army base, the center now hosts schools, churches, non-profit organizations and outdoor schools.

The campus also offers lodging in luxurious accommodations that was once the base officer's quarters.

Ft. Casey State Park and a portion of Camp Casey, operated by Seattle Pacific University (below), taken March 2006; Ft. Casey coast line (facing page) taken March 2006.

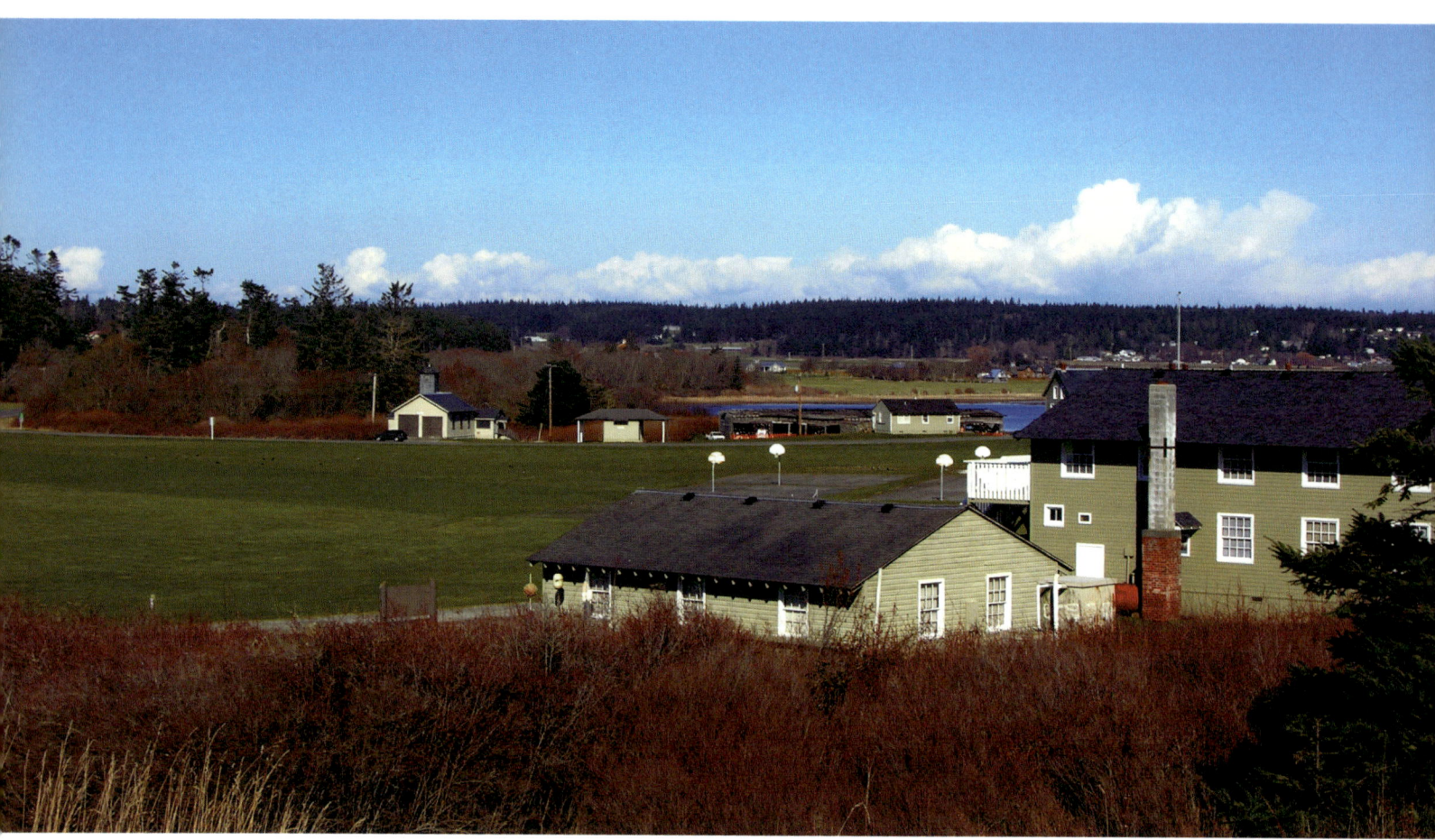

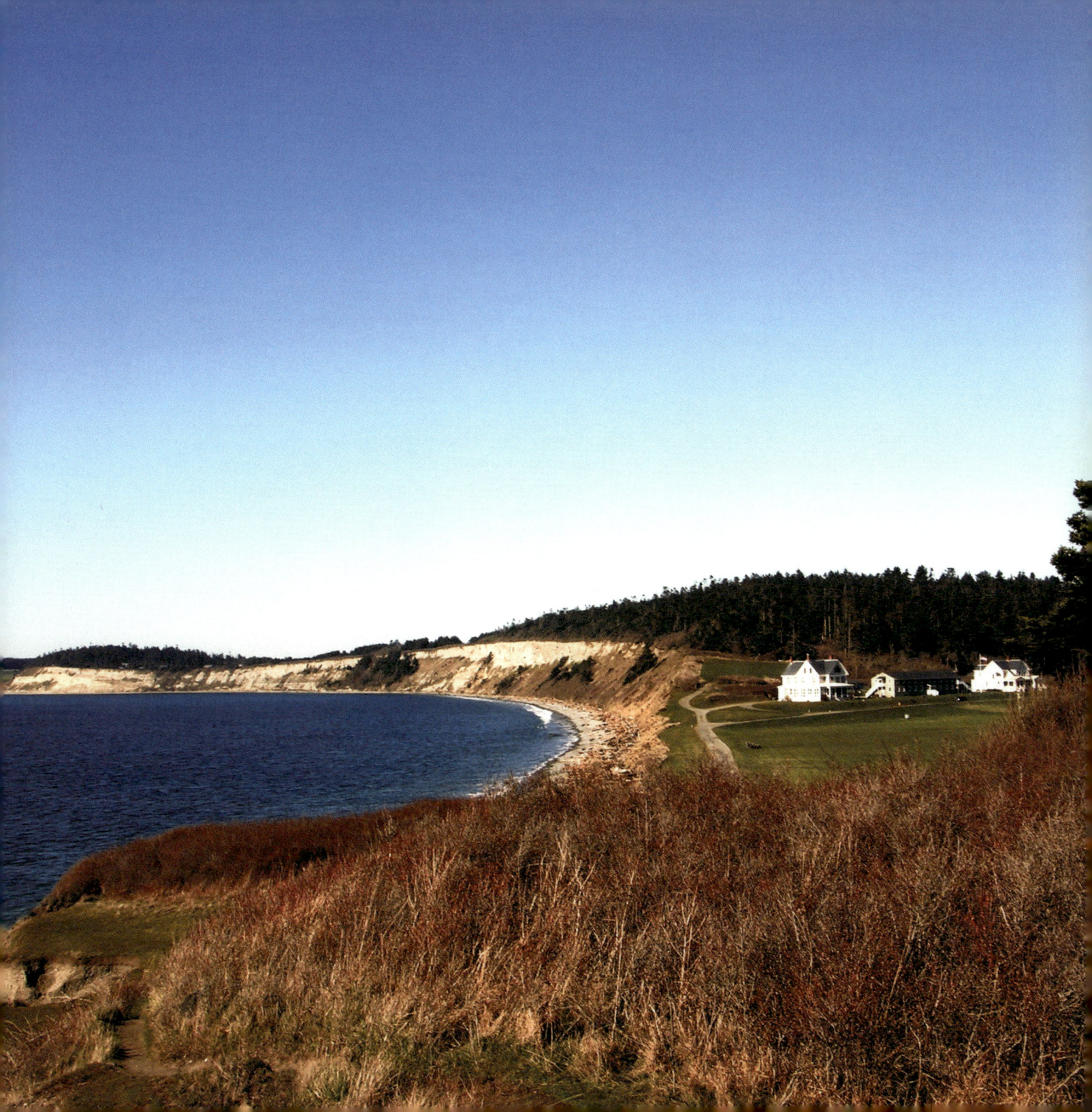

Greenbank

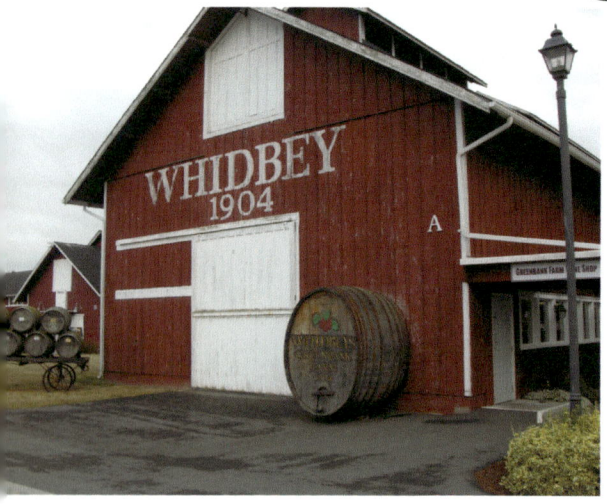

Greenbank Farm is more than a farm. It's a restaurant, art galleries, antique shops, location for a farmer's market and arts and crafts shows.

Located on the narrowest point of Whidbey Island, South of Coupeville and North of Freeland, Greenbank Farm consists of over 500 acres of rolling hills, forests, and ponds.

Park your alpaca and taste some of the treats offered by Whidbey Island, enjoy the crafts and history and, of course, the view.

For more information, visit:
www.greenbankfarm.com

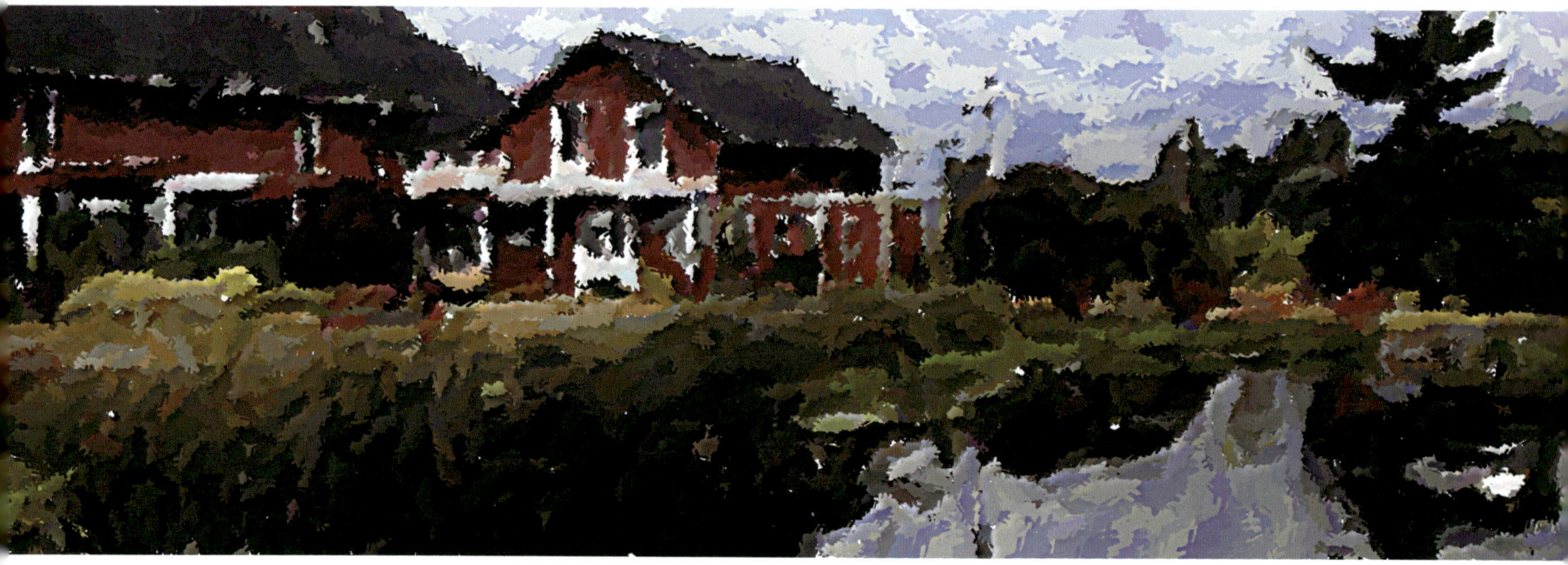

Greenbank Farm (above, below and facing page) taken Sept. 2006

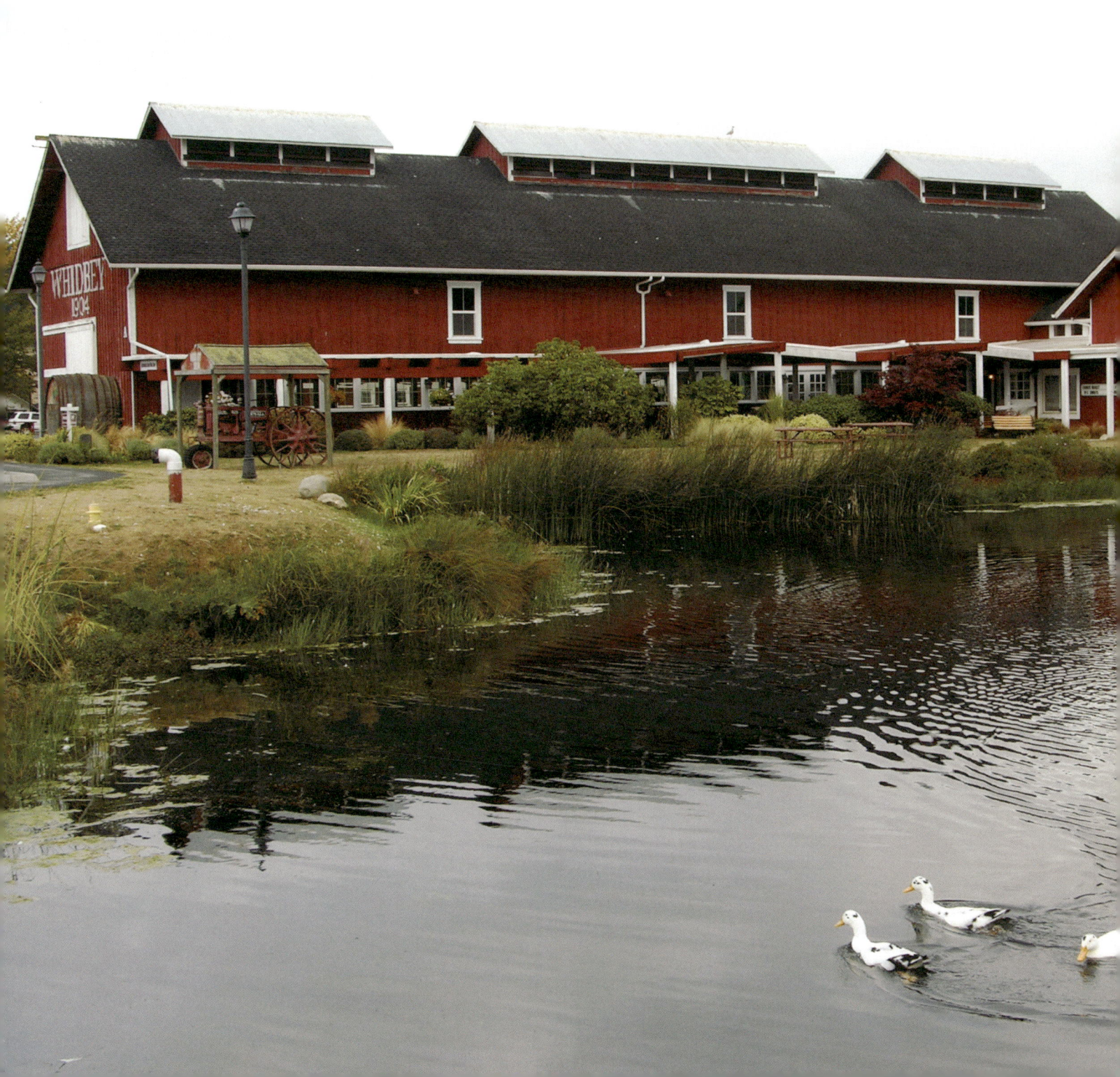

Freeland

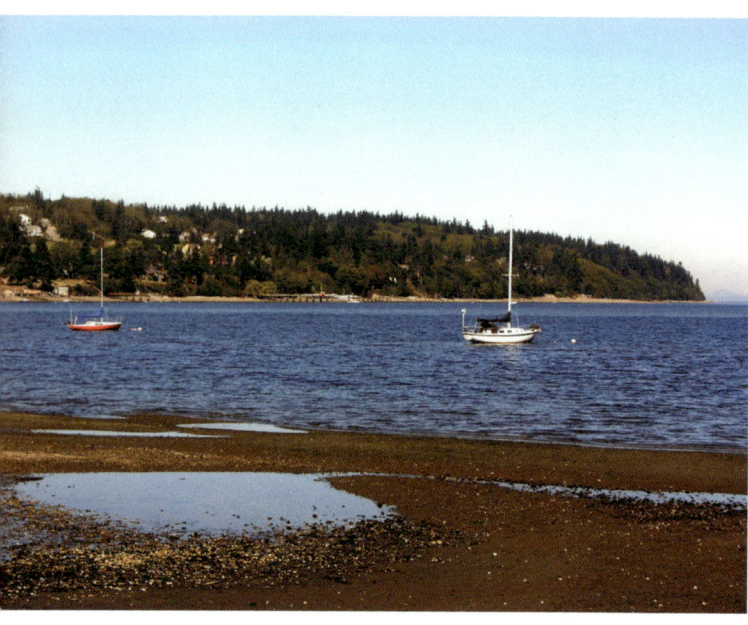

The Town of Freeland was incorporated in 1900 by a group of Socialists who wanted to create a utopia of a sorts.

Located at the South end of Holmes Harbor, its idyllic location pretty much assured its founders' utopian aspirations.

Today, Freeland is a tourist and commerce center for Southern Whidbey Island. There are a variety of shops, restaurants, accommodations, and a wonderful harbor-front park.

All photos on this and facing page taken Sept. 2006 in Freeland.

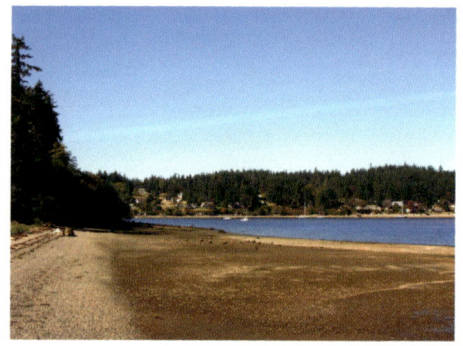
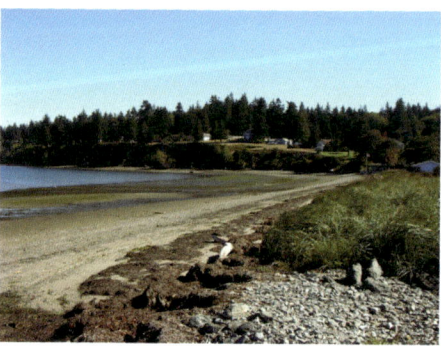
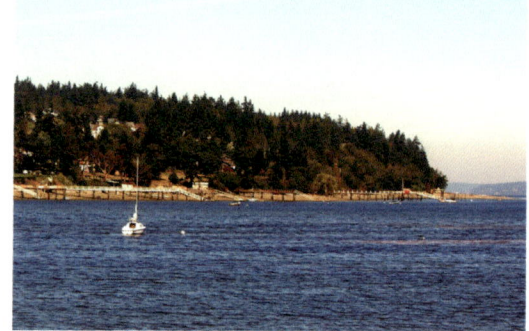

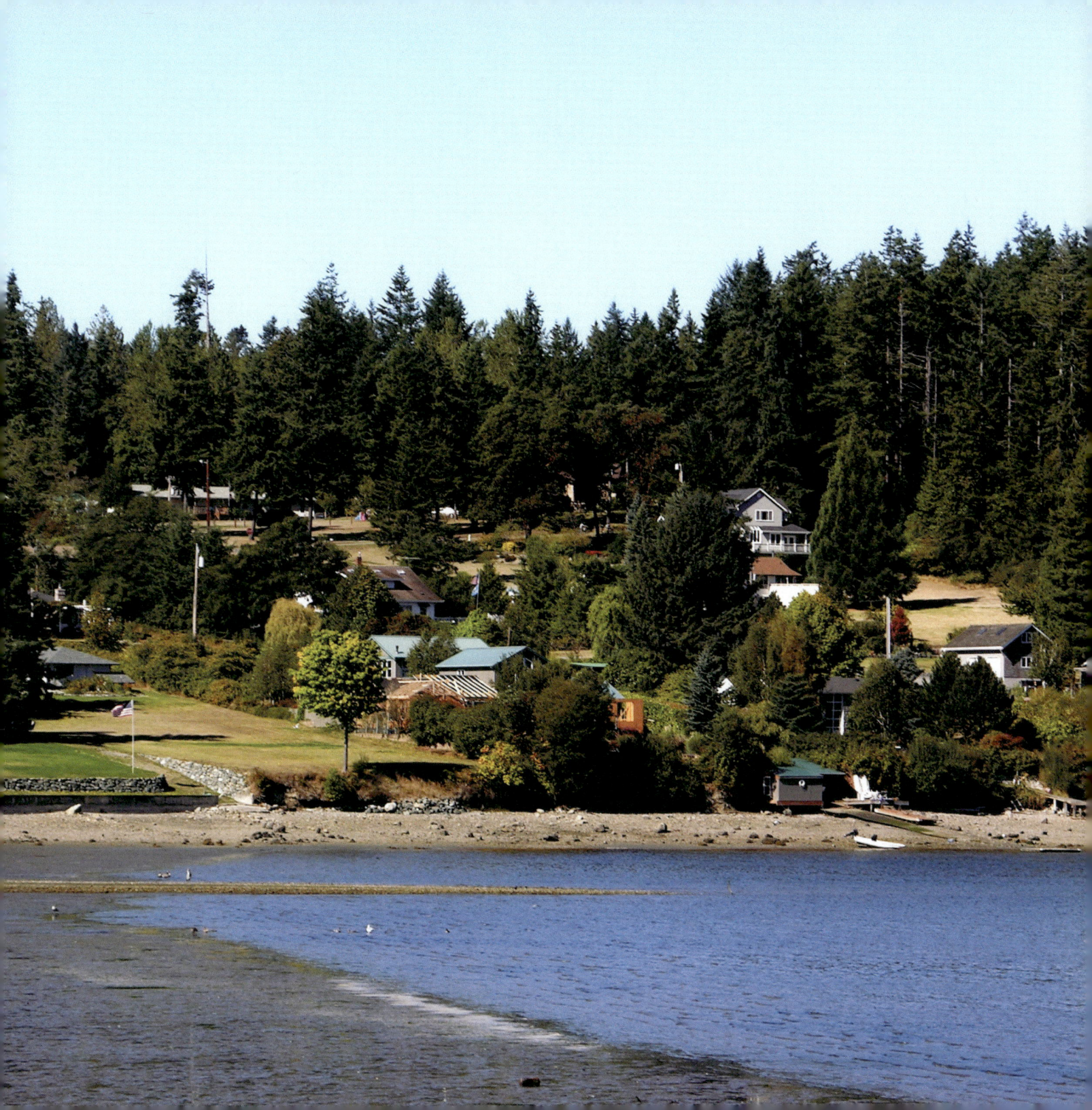

Double Bluff Park

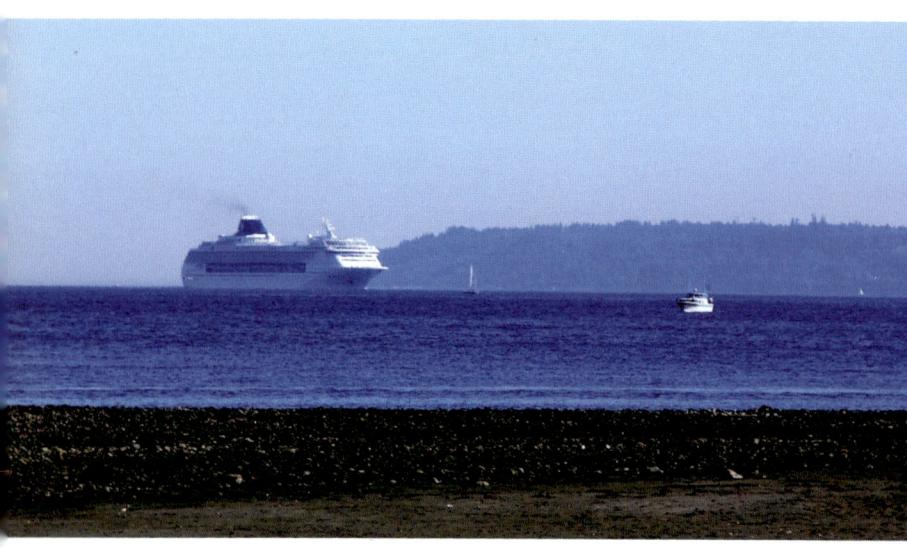

Double Bluff Park is located almost due South of Freeland on the edge of Useless Bay.

High bluffs, sandy beaches, wildlife, and a leash-free area for dogs, Double Bluff Park is a wonderful family area.

And on a clear day, you can see Seattle and Mt. Rainier.

All photos on this page and facing page taken Aug. 2006

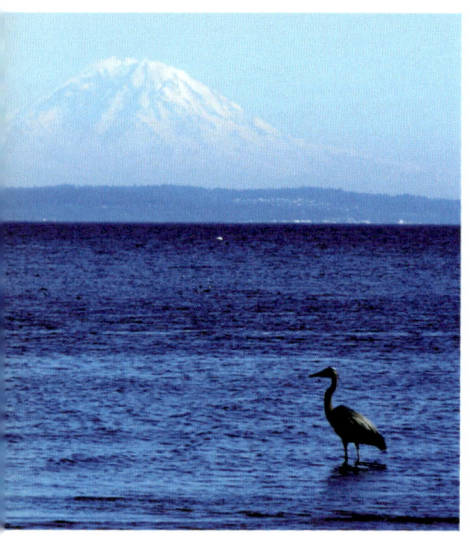
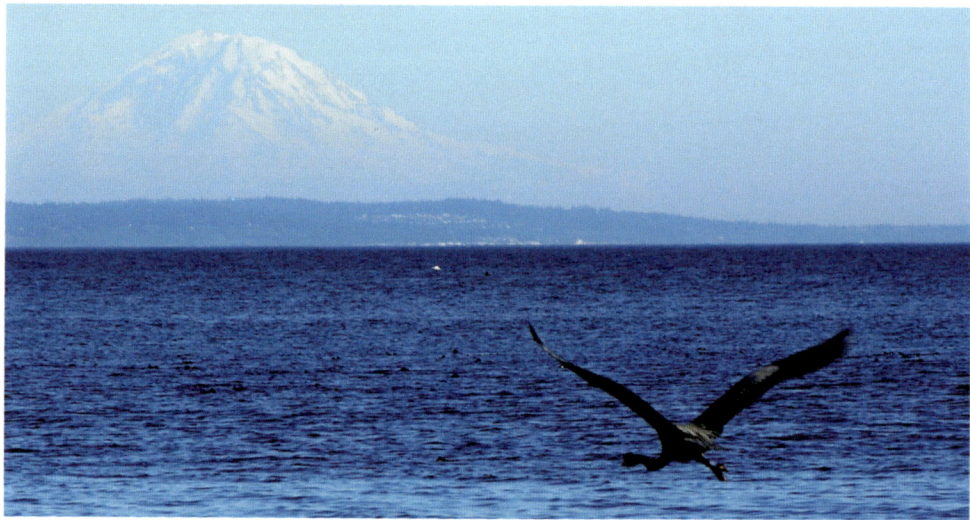

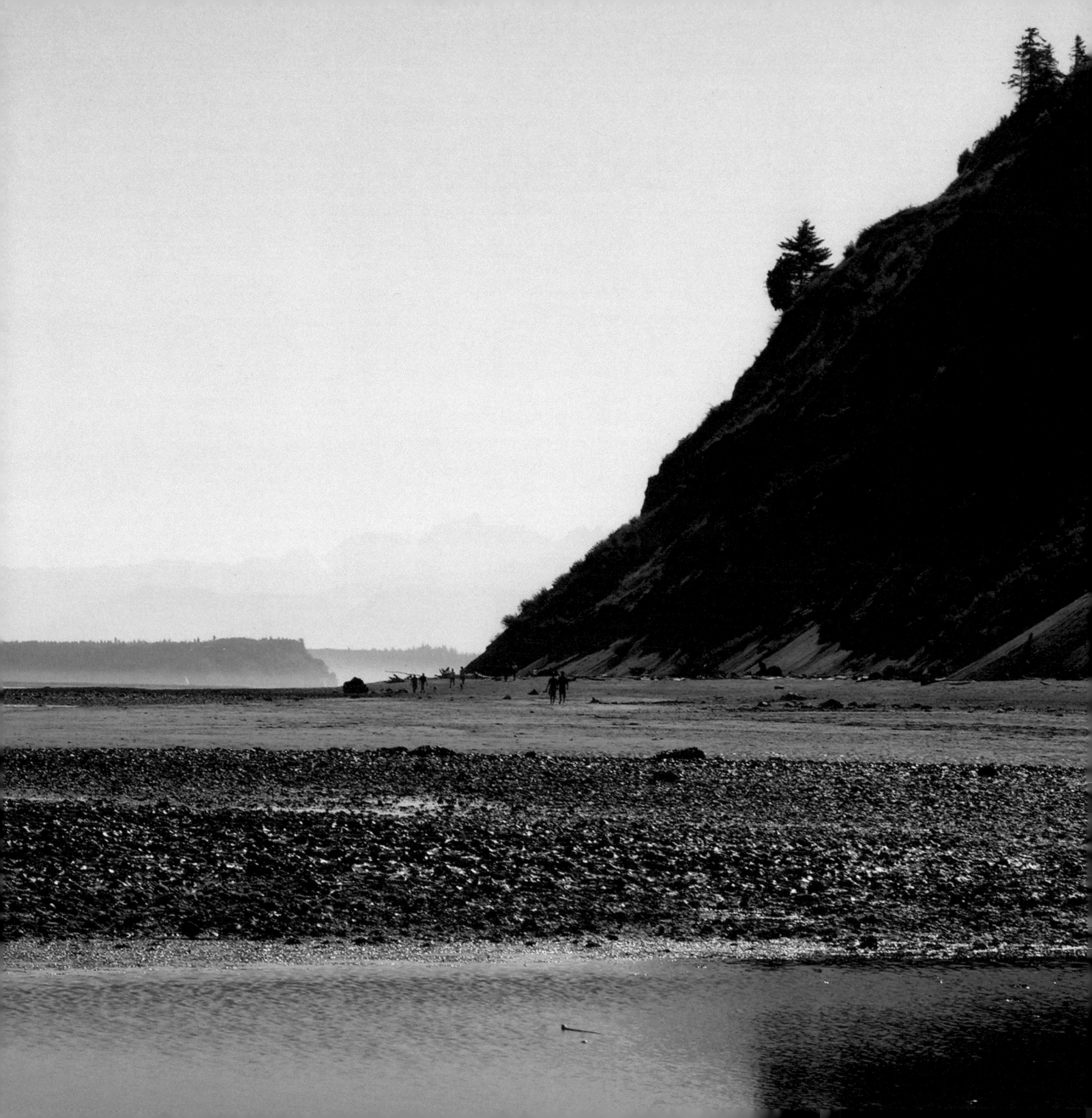

Langley

Langley has been compared to Carmel, California as it was in the 50s. Incorporated in 1913, Langley retains its small town look and feel.

Home of many artists, fine dining, and intriguing shops, Langley is a top tourist destination. It boasts many bed and breakfasts, inns, and cottages.

Located North of Clinton on the edge of the Saratoga Passage and Possession Sound, Langley offers spectacular sights from its waterfront parks and overlooks.

Langley is also site of the annual Island County Fair.

Year around activities make Langley an unforgettable destination—one that will live on in fond memories for years to come.

From Langley looking East (below) taken March, 2006; Langley sculpture (facing page) taken Sept. 2006.

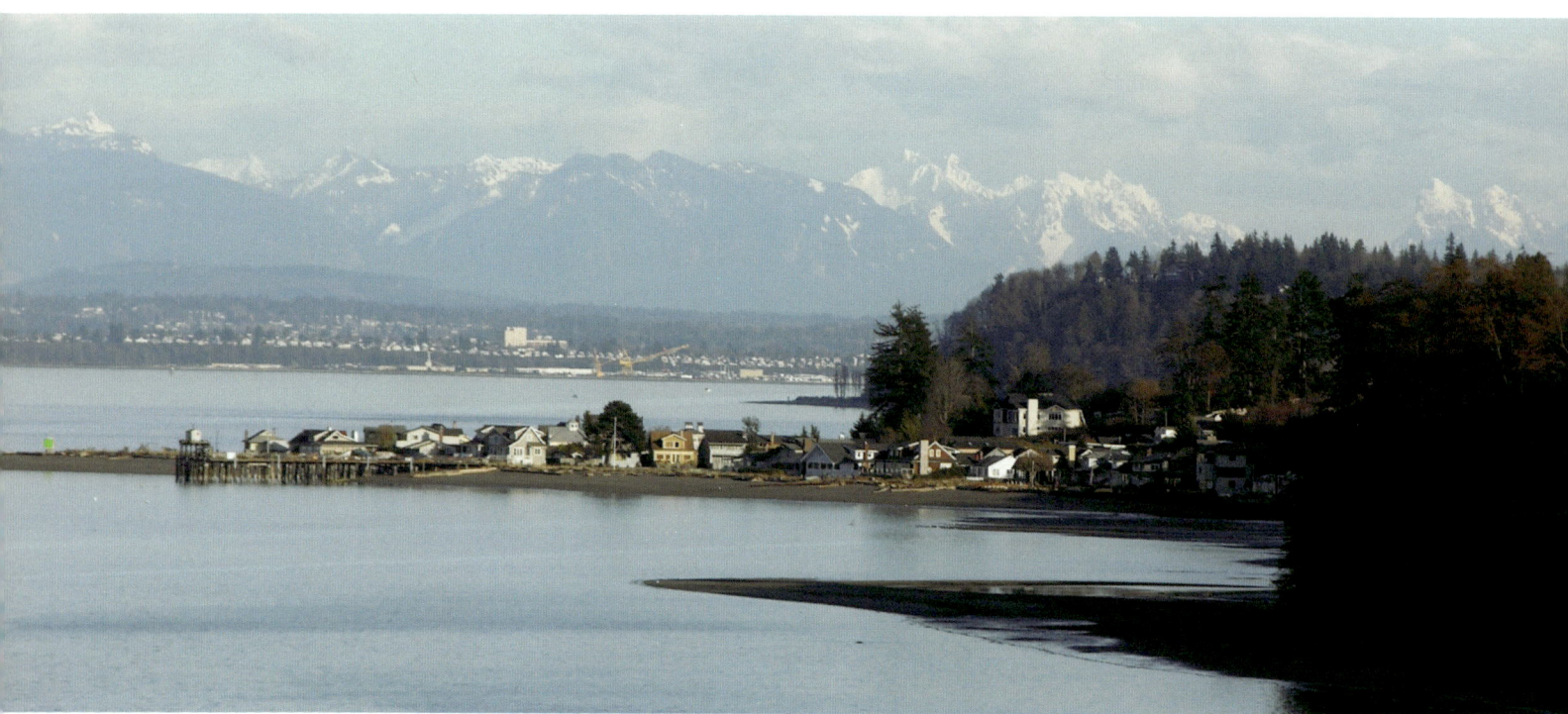

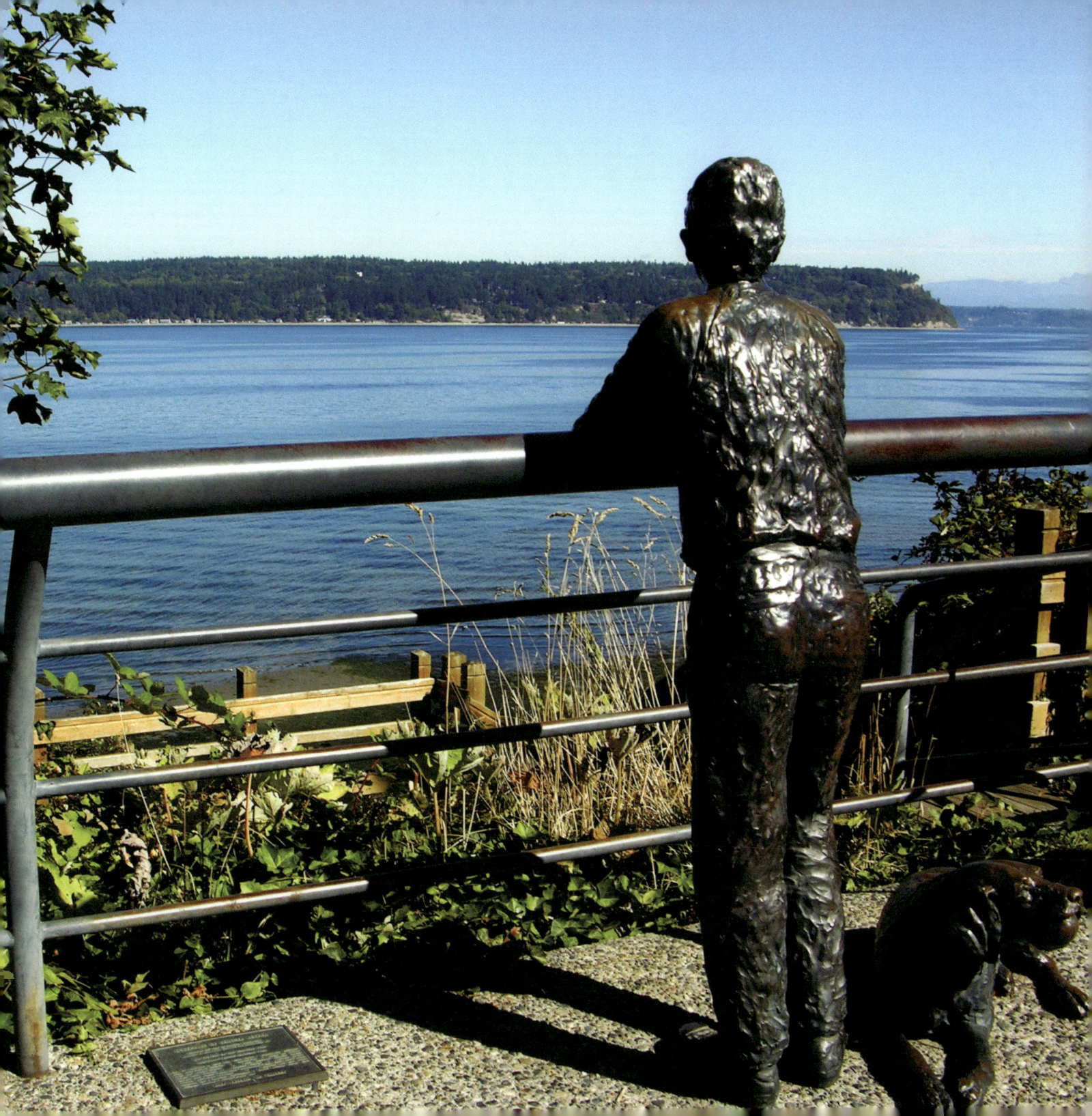

Langley

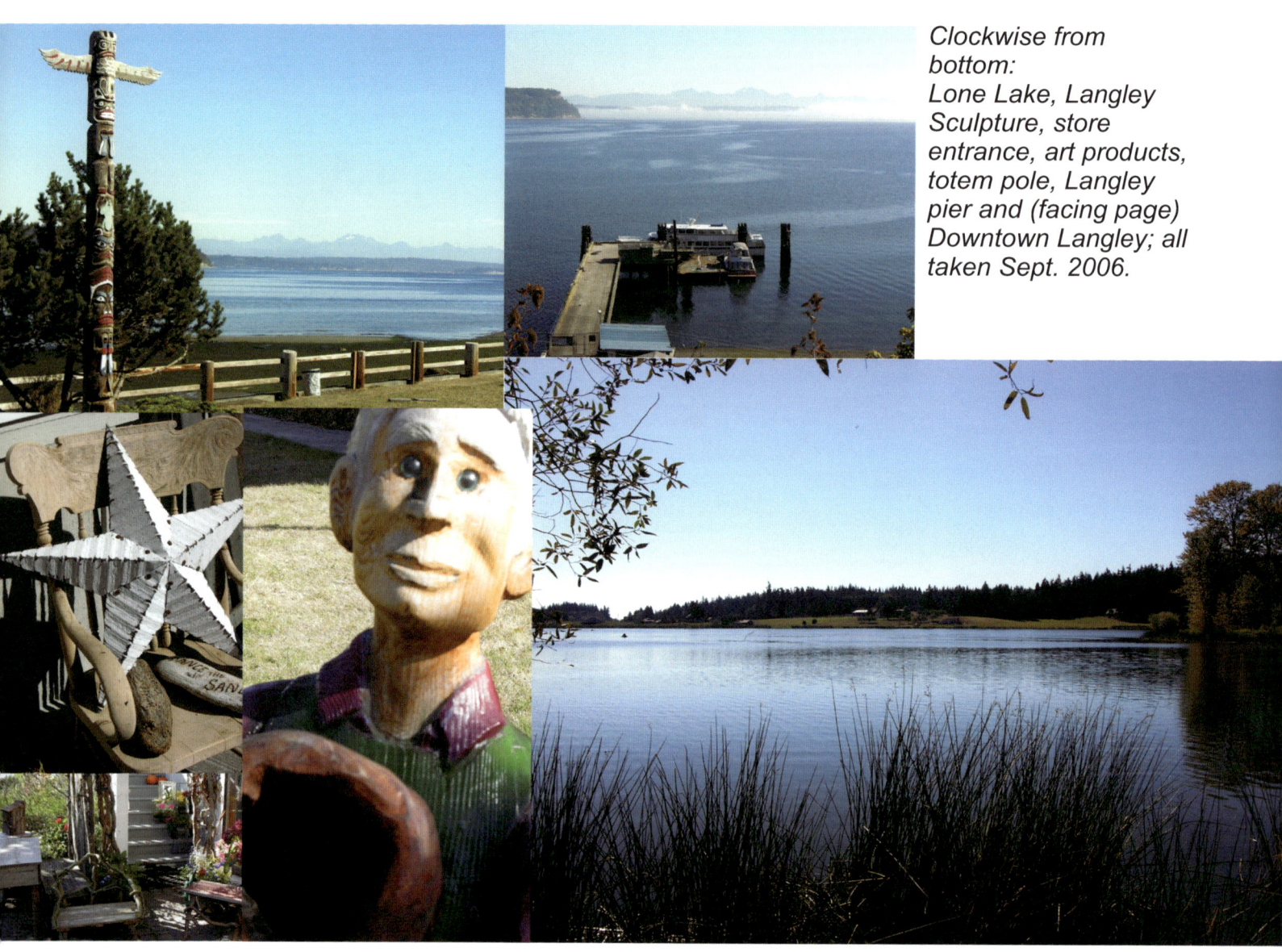

Clockwise from bottom: Lone Lake, Langley Sculpture, store entrance, art products, totem pole, Langley pier and (facing page) Downtown Langley; all taken Sept. 2006.

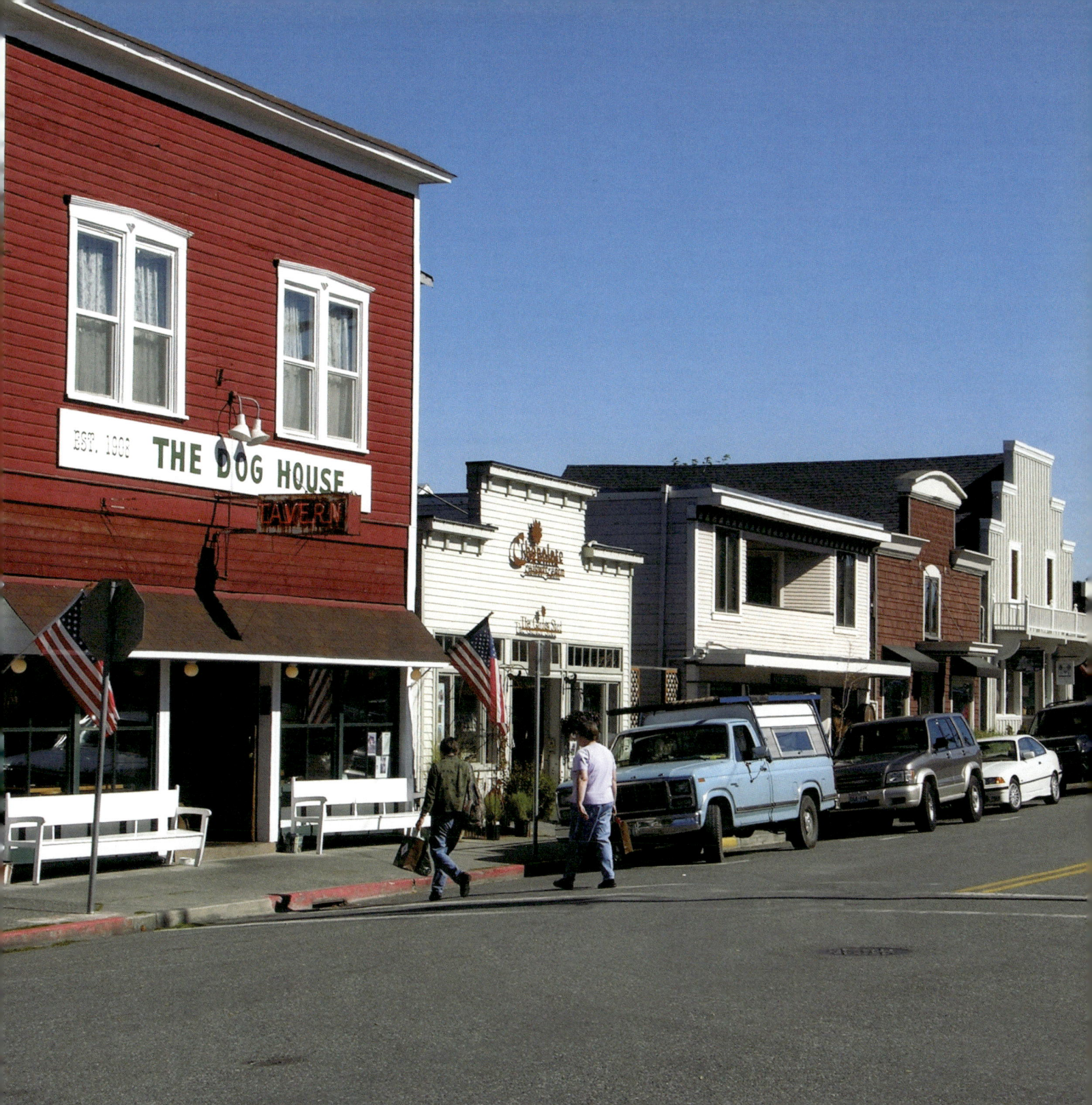

Clinton

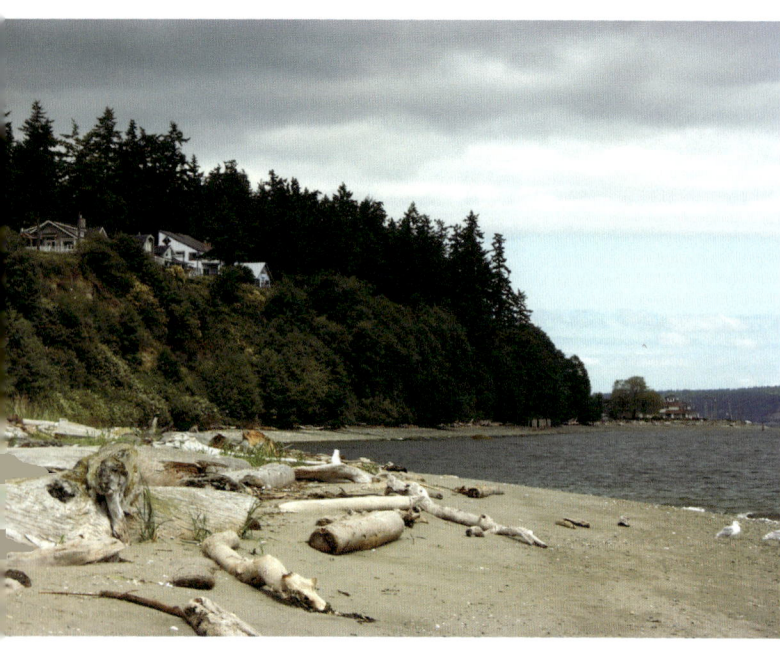

Clinton is the first community many visitors to Whidbey see as they arrive at the island on the Mukilteo-Clinton Ferry.

Clinton serves at the commercial hub for the Southern area of Whidbey. Check out the neat mini-park next to the Ferry terminal.

Seeing the homes on the beach as one arrives at Whidbey serves to enhance the magic of this magical place.

You know, as the Ferry kisses the edge of Whidbey, you've left the rest of the world behind.

Clinton beach (above); Ferry terminal (below), and park (facing page), all taken July, 2006.

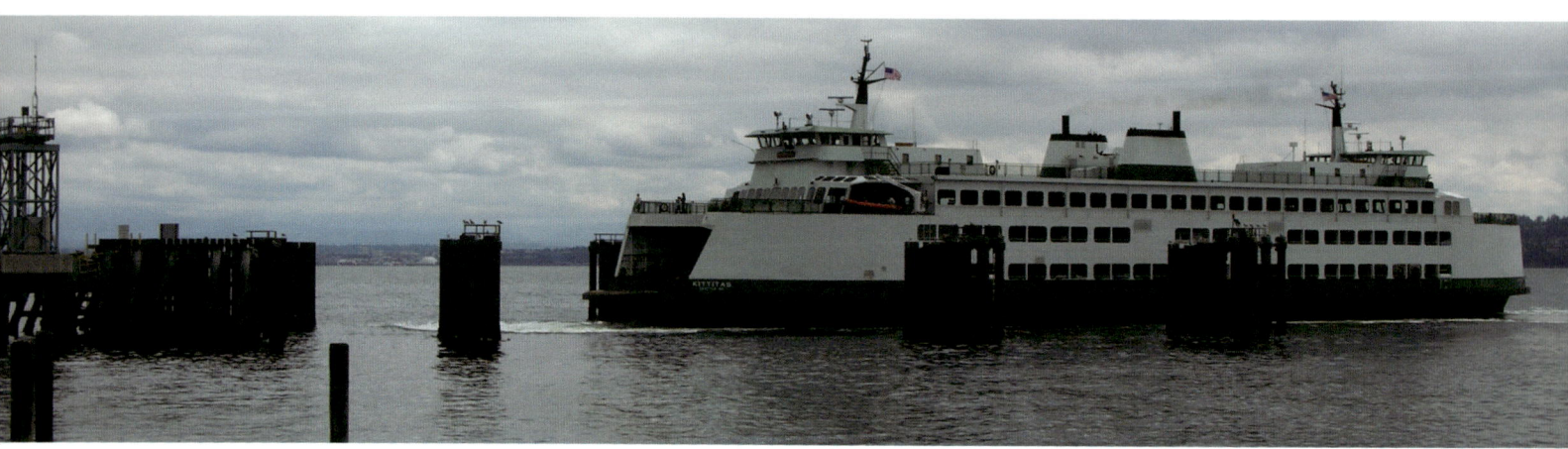

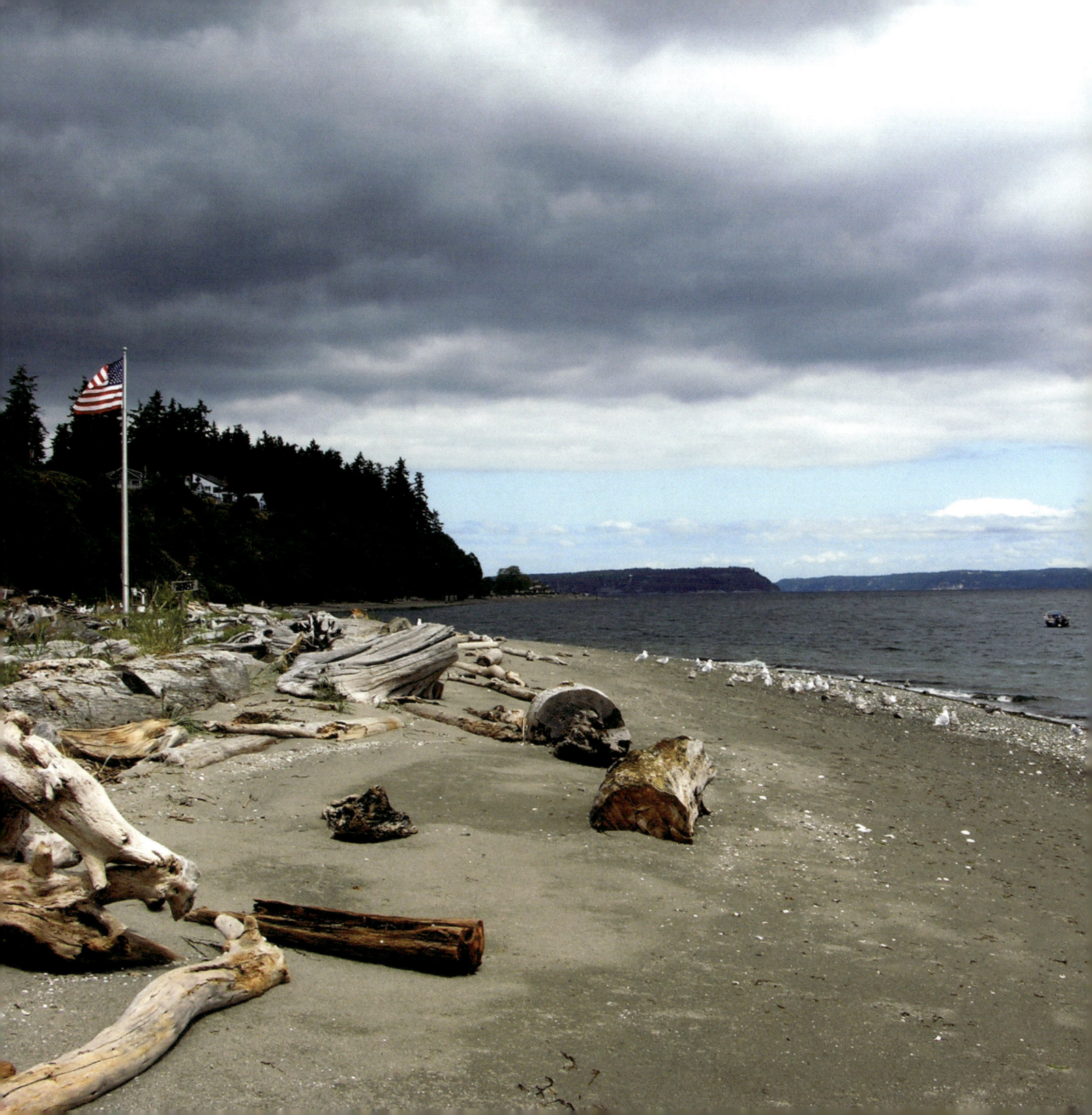

Whidbey Island Flora

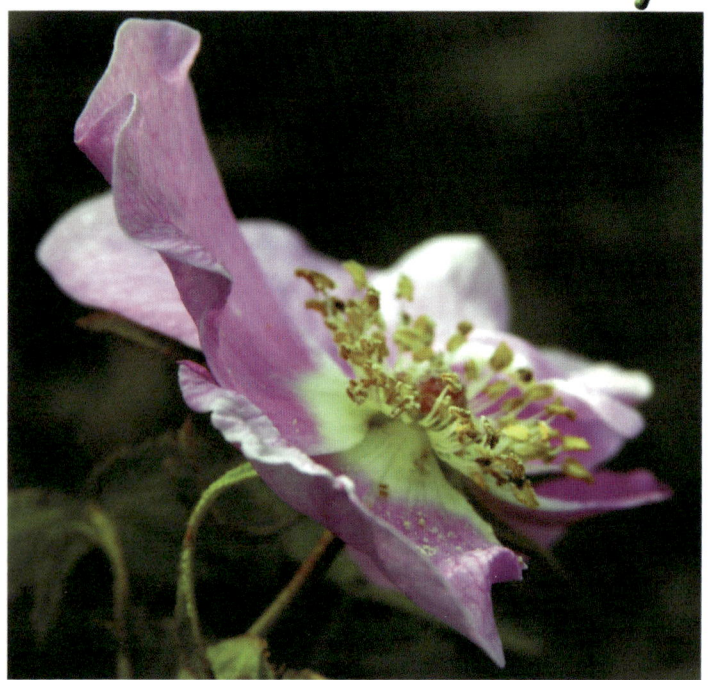
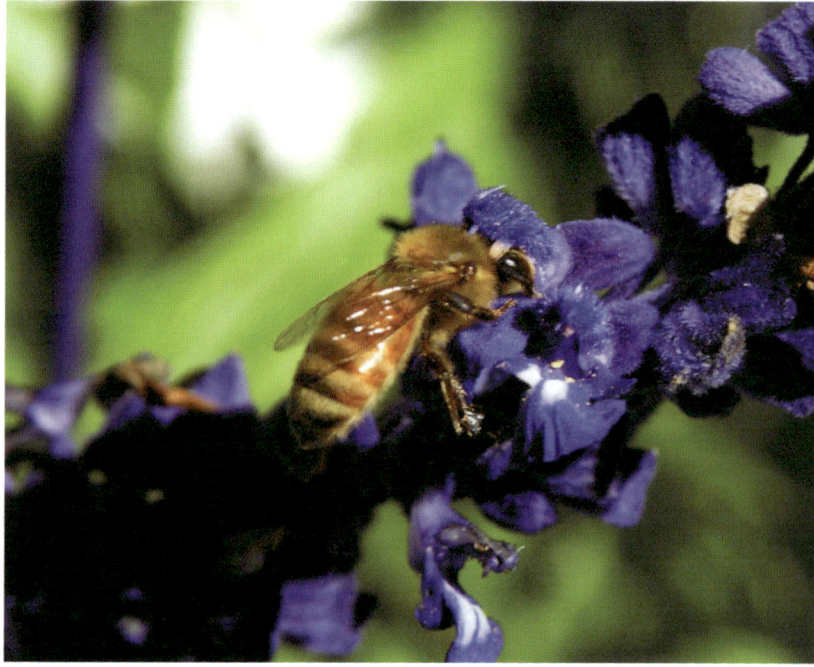

Not being a botanist, a flourintologist, a horticulturist, or even a very good speller, the author is not sure what types of plants are represented on this page. He only knows they attracted him because of their, well — attractiveness.

Above left was taken March, 2006; the remainder were taken Sept. 2006.

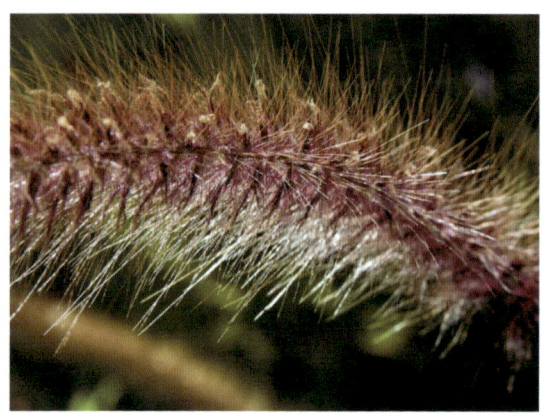
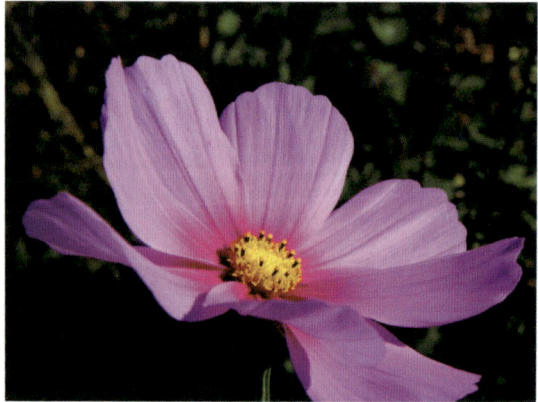
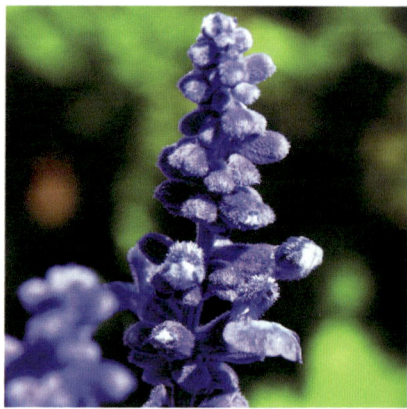

About the Author

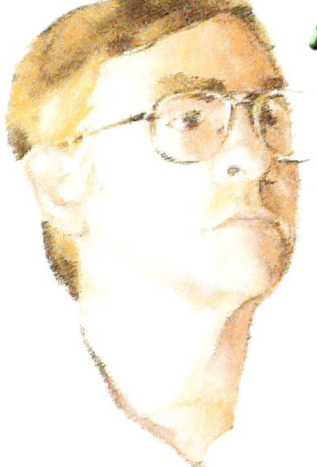

Rick Lawler is an avid photographer, an adequate graphic designer, and an okay writer.

He wrote, published, and sold over 25,000 copies of How to Contact World Leaders, which he updated and published annually from 1990 until 2004; 55,000 copies of Owner to Owner: Guide to WorldMark Ownership, a best selling timeshare book that was first published in 2002 and updated annually.

Lawler administers web sites www.minref.com his MinRef Press publishing site and www.gopnw.com, Go Pacific Northwest, a site that offers souvenirs and other products of the Pacific Northwest featuring Lawler's photos and graphic design.

He resides in Oak Harbor on beautiful Whidbey Island with his family: Spouse Alice, daughter Sara, and son Sean.

Note on photographs: Photos have been modified to the following extent: Contrast and brightness have been adjusted to offer the most pleasing and realistic presentation, then cropped to fit the available space. One photo, Downtown Langley on Page 35, had many utility lines removed (if you look closely, you can discern where the lines originally appeared).

Local Whidbey Island Links (subject to change):
www.islandcountytourism.com or www.whidbeycamanoislands.com
www.islandhistory.org — Island County Historical Society
www.oakharborchamber.org – www.centralwhidbeychamber.com
www.langleychamber.com

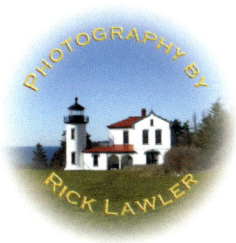

Special Thanks to:
RoseAnn Alspektor, Marketing Coordinator for **Island County Tourism** for her kind support and advice.
Oak Harbor Seventh-day Adventist Church, 31830 SR 20, Oak Harbor for being a wonderfully supportive church family.
Kapaw's Iskreme, 21 NW Front St, Coupeville, for the best cones.
Whidbey Island Bank for their friendly service.
Whidbey Island Writers Association for making me a winner.
Imperial, 33505 SR 20, Oak Harbor for the best Chinese food.
The Mad Crab, 10 NW Front St, Coupeville for great fish and chips.
Sno-Isle Library, 1000 SE Regatta Dr, Oak Harbor for books and movies.
Mike's Place, 219 1st, Langley for great family food.
Casa Rodriguez, 705 SE Pioneer Way, Oak Harbor, our lunch favorite.

Printed in the United States
151929LV00001B